D1546579

"Why should I stand behind the *mechitzah* when I could be a prayer leader?"

"Why should I stand behind the *mechitzah* when I could be a prayer leader?"

The Traditional Jewish Response for the Contemporary Woman

Marina Goodman

TARGUM/FELDHEIM

First published 2002
Copyright © 2002 by Marina Goodman
ISBN 1-56871-217-0

Published by:
TARGUM PRESS, INC.
22700 W. Eleven Mile Rd.
Southfield, MI 48034
E-mail: targum@netvision.net.il
Fax: 888-298-9992
www.targum.com

Distributed by:
FELDHEIM PUBLISHERS
202 Airport Executive Park
Nanuet, NY 10954

Printed in Israel

Rabbi Zev Leff

Rabbi of Moshav Matityahu
Rosh Hayeshiva Yeshiva Gedola Matisyahu
D. N. Modi'in 71917 Tel. (08) 976-1138 Fax. (08) 976-5326

I have read the manuscript of *"Why Should I Stand Behind the Mechitzah When I Could be a Prayer Leader?": The Traditional Response for the Contemporary Woman* by Mrs. Marina Goodman.

The author presents a very interesting approach to the role of a woman in Torah and mitzvos. The presentation is both intellectually stimulating and emotionally inspiring. The personal notes and insights that highlight the author's own life's experiences in her quest and growth in Torah serve as a source of strength, encouragement, and guidance for all those involved in a similar quest.

I would like to point out that this is a work for the contemporary woman, as indicated by the subtitle. Women of previous generations did not need this type of work, because these issues were self-evident to them, absorbed into their very being by the osmosis of Jewish tradition and the intensity of the Jewish home. Contemporary circumstances and the confusion caused by "modern" philosophies not compatible with Torah make a work as this necessary. An important point to keep in mind when reading this work is that a true Torah Jew is motivated in fulfilling the role that will enable them to fulfill God's will and not that which will make them feel fulfilled. We live in a world where one's main focus is the latter — a very selfish, self-centered attitude. The Torah guides us to find our fulfillment in fulfilling our God-given responsibilities.

Although I do not know Mrs. Goodman personally, I am told by Torah personalities who are acquainted with her that she is a devoted wife and mother who is committed to Torah and mitzvos.

I highly recommend this book to both women and men who would want to get a clear understanding of the role of women in Judaism, from the author's viewpoint. This viewpoint reflects one of the legitimate Torah perspectives on this issue.

May Hashem bless the author and her family with life and health and the ability to continue to merit the community with her Torah knowledge and as a positive role model.

With Torah blessings,
Sincerely,

Rabbi Zev Leff

Congregation Ahavas Achim   phone   732 247 0532
216 South First Avenue   fax   732 247 6739
P.O. Box 4242   email   rabbi@ahavasachim.org
Highland Park, NJ 08904   web   www.ahavaachim.org

June 7, 2002
27 Sivan, 5762

Dear reader,

The modern era has seen fundamental and widespread changes in society's value system. Occasionally, this value system conflicts with and sometimes even contradicts that of our holy Torah. One example is the diametrically opposing views of modernity and traditional Judaism regarding the role of women in almost every aspect of life.

This insightful book will introduce the open-minded reader to refreshing new perspectives on the most troubling issues confronting the modern and enlightened women vis-à-vis her Judaism. Mrs. Goodman draws upon her own religious odyssey, as well as countless Biblical and Rabbinic sources, to demonstrate the timeless nature and virtuous role of Jewish women.

It was a privilege to witness the evolution of this book. I strongly recommend it to anyone — male or famale — who wishes to better his or her understanding and comprehension of one of the most misunderstood areas of Judaism in the modern era.

With blessings of Torah,

Rabbi Ronald L. Schwarzberg

Dedication

to my parents and
to every woman who
searches for Truth

Contents

Acknowledgments

I am so grateful to my parents, Mark and Bella Zelkin, who did everything for me and made sure I always had the very best of what was important in life — their unconditional love and an excellent education. Everything I have become, even when it was not what they expected, is only because of them.

I am also very thankful to my teacher in Jerusalem, Blima Moskoff. From her I learned the beauty of modesty and so much more. It was because of her patience, constancy, warmth, and wisdom that I became a *baalat teshuvah*. A big thanks also to all the people who reached out to me and others and invited us into their homes.

My wonderful husband has supported me throughout in my every endeavor. He never told me that I can't do something. I will always be grateful to him for his patience, guidance, and comments. He was the sounding board for many of my ideas and his questions have challenged me to refine them.

Much thanks goes to my miracle baby, who has taught me so much about Hashem's ways.

I very much appreciate all of Rabbi Schwarzberg's efforts to make sure that the manuscript was accurate from both a halachic and hashkafic standpoint. He took the time from his hectic schedule of being a community leader to carefully go over the book and offer his insightful comments.

I want to thank Gila Manolson for her indispensable help in making this book a reality.

When I was in deep spiritual darkness, Sarah Idit Schneider shone a light on the spiritual path I needed to follow, and for this I will always be grateful.

I am grateful to Marianna Vulakh and Cheryl Farkas for carefully reviewing the manuscript, and to Andrew Farkas for getting me certain key, hard-to-find books.

I am thankful to Arthur Kurzweil and his staff for challenging me to expand and concretize the book.

Finally, I thank Hashem for giving me the strength to get through each day.

Introduction

Before Beginning...

Being Jewish can be very painful for a woman. Standing behind the *mechitzah*, the separation in the synagogue between men and women, while the men worship God in ways that Jewish law says she never can, makes her feel irrelevant and robbed. Not being counted in a minyan, the quorum of ten men necessary for public worship, confirms her belief that women just do not count in Judaism. But this is not some other religion where some other women don't count. It is "my religion" and "I don't count." She feels like she is being rejected by something that is rightfully hers. This pain leads to outrage. At this point a woman has two choices. One is to reject the parts of Judaism she does not like as antiquated and change rituals according to her beliefs. The second choice is to learn. However, in order to learn one must be a good student.

Who would you think is the "good" student? Is she the one dutifully absorbing unquestioningly everything her teacher tells her, and knowing all the correct answers? Or is she the one who is struggling with the material and constantly asking questions? The Talmud teaches us something completely counterintuitive,

"A person does not really integrate words of Torah unless he at first stumbles over them."[1] The former type of student will get an A in her class. The latter type of student has the potential to acquire Torah. Let us look more closely at how this happens.

When the Jews received the Torah at Mount Sinai, they did not just receive a piece of parchment with ink, they also had the Torah engraved onto their hearts. Each one of us has the entire Torah within us! Problems arise when the "outer" Torah seems to conflict with our "inner" Torah.[2] Imagine that you are a traveler and you need to find the way to your destination. You find several pathways, but they all have closed gates in front of them. You look around again to find some open gates and realize that there are none. If you want to get to your destination, then you only have one choice: figure out a way to open one of these gates. Do you have problems with the Torah? Good! You have found your closed gates that will lead you to acquiring Torah.

How do you go about opening these gates? There are three things that you need to do. The first is to keep an open mind. Assume that an acceptable resolution exists. Be open to new ideas and new information. It is not enough to just pose a question, you must also actively listen to the response.

For a Jew to learn about Judaism poses many difficulties. The biggest one is the assumption that one already understands the Jewish outlook. This makes it very difficult to keep an open mind. If one were to seriously study a culture that one knows nothing about, the very "strangeness" of the culture would be a constant reminder of one's ignorance and the importance of learning with an open mind without passing judgments. Famil-

---

1 *Gittin* 43:2.
2 Sarah Schneider, *A Still Small Voice*, Synchrony Lesson 9 (Jerusalem: 1988), 2.

iarity with a culture, even on a superficial level, has the opposite effect. It's too easy to think that one knows enough to draw conclusions. An example of this is how easily people can jump to discriminatory conclusions about minority groups that they constantly see but with whom they have no intimate contact.

Family get-togethers for Rosh HaShanah and for the Passover seder, a trip to Israel, and supporting Jewish causes certainly gives one a sense of Jewish identity and Jewish values. However, being immersed in American society and inundated with its value system changes one's frame of reference. We then look at Judaism through the biased lens of a foreign value system. Judaism thus looks strange indeed. Our familiarity leads us to believe that our interpretations of what we see are correct and no further questioning is necessary. And yet this is where the questions should begin, for here the learning starts.

As an example, suppose one lives in culture A where red is associated with men and white is associated with women. Red has traditionally also been considered a superior color to white. In recent years, proponents of equality have championed the belief that red is just as much a color for women as it is for men. Much progress has been made and red has become much more associated with women.

Then one looks at culture B where red is associated with men and white is associated with women. What is one to think of culture B? One's first reaction may be that culture B is sexist and backwards, and that someone living in culture A has nothing to learn from it. However, without further investigation, this is not a fair assessment of culture B. It may be that red and white are considered equally beautiful colors. Assigning red to men and white to women is therefore not an indication of sexism.

But then why not be egalitarian and assign both colors to

both men and women? Why not just have one color? Perhaps in culture B, each color is considered unique and necessary to achieve complete beauty. Therefore, one cannot simply eliminate one or substitute one with another. Assigning a color to a gender may be a ramification of culture B's theories on gender. Judging by the beliefs about the colors, the genders are considered different, irreplaceable, beautiful, and equal.

Once one has an open mind and is ready to learn, another problem arises. It is easy to ask, "What is a religion's value system?" When faced with one's own religion, however, one must also struggle with the question, "Do I believe in this value system?" At this point the challenge begins. Keep in mind that these are two separate questions and not to judge so quickly.

One's personal beliefs on colors must be temporarily suspended and one must keep an open and inquisitive mind if one is to fairly assess culture B. Then one can wrestle with how culture B's beliefs compare with one's own. One may find that white is indeed just as beautiful a color as red. The fight for equality in culture A was noble but misplaced. Maybe learning from culture B would inspire one to fight for the equality between the colors.

The second thing you must do in order to open your gate is to examine your own position.[1] First articulate the problem. What exactly do I have a conflict with? Then think critically about your position. Where does this belief come from? Is this something that I have just accepted from society? Or does this come from the depths of my heart?

The third thing you need to do is to look again at the "outer" Torah.[2] Do I have all the facts? A common mistake is to only read

---

1   Ibid., 3.
2   Ibid.

the written Torah without taking into consideration the oral Torah. The most famous example of this is the common phrase "an eye for an eye, a tooth for a tooth." The Jewish court never gouged out anybody's eye or knocked out anybody's tooth. This was meant metaphorically to signify that monetary payments be made if one physically harmed another person in accordance with the harm done.

My goal with this book is to help with this third step. However, the first two steps are up to you.

Opening these gates and acquiring Torah is a lifelong process of self-transformation. As Sarah Schneider writes:

> Those practices and/or assertions of Torah that you doubt or resist become your points of stumbling. But if you struggle with them and insist upon a satisfying resolution, and search and question until you find an answer that truly satisfies your soul, then everything turns upside down and those become the areas of Torah that are yours in a deeply integrated way. They become your doorway into the depths of its teachings. They become your most solid ground, the things that you will teach to others, and upon which you will base your life.[1]

Learning about Judaism is a constant wrestling with oneself. Each woman will have her own questions to which she will have to find her own answers. No one book will tell her everything she wants to know, and no amount of reading books will help her understand everything there is to Judaism. The most important lessons can only be learned through action and observation.

Here we will examine a few of the most common problems

---

1   Ibid., 2.

that women have with Judaism. These are the solutions that I have found in my struggle with what it means to be an Orthodox Jewish woman. These are not the only answers, so if you don't like them — keep asking!

Personal Reflections

My family only went to the synagogue twice a year — on Rosh HaShanah and Yom Kippur. We were originally from the Soviet Union and there the terms *Reform*, *Conservative*, and *Orthodox* had no meaning. Therefore, the synagogue we attended was chosen based on proximity, and this happened to be Orthodox.

One Yom Kippur during my freshman year in college, it all just got to me. I went to the synagogue to catch *Kol Nidrei*. I stood in the back of the balcony with the other women, barely making out the words of the strange song the cantor was singing. I couldn't see anything unless I leaned forward directly over the railing. Women were talking and running after children. Many didn't concentrate on the prayers because they knew that it just didn't matter whether they were even there. I felt like Jewish tradition made me a spectator. The overpowering feeling of marginality overwhelmed me and I ran out of the shul in tears, promising myself that I would never return.

At college I joined a Conservative egalitarian minyan that met Friday nights. A group of around forty students and faculty members filled a room in Anabel Taylor Hall, and we lifted our souls and voices in harmonized song as the setting sun beamed at us in blues and golds through the stained glass. By sophomore year, I was one of the people who led services. As long as I concentrated on prayer, I didn't feel self-conscious and sang well. Afterwards, during Kiddush, many people complimented me on my beautiful voice.

In my junior year I studied in Israel at Hebrew University in Jerusalem during the fall semester. I knew I was so ignorant about Judaism that I didn't even know what I didn't know. My goal was to learn so much that I would at least realize what questions to ask. There were three topics I wanted to learn about: Judaism, Jewish history, and what it meant to live in Israel. Religion, I decided, was best learned from the religious. The academia seemed to do everything they could to tear it apart and reduce it to some primitive oddity. I wanted to learn from those who loved it.

While I was in college, my weekly attendance at the Friday night services and then the dinner at the kosher dining hall became a habit. Slowly, I realized that my life developed a weekly rhythm with the Sabbath as its highlight. This was something I would never have realized, much less appreciated, had I tried to understand the Sabbath in a purely cerebral manner. This was one of my first lessons in Judaism: sometimes the only way to understand something is to do it.

When I went to Israel, I decided to put this lesson into practice. There was a lot I didn't understand in Judaism, including why I should keep kosher and how it was possible to keep the Sabbath not only Friday nights but Saturday days as well. Before I went to Israel, I decided that during my stay there I would keep kosher, observe the Sabbath both Friday night and Saturday day, and learn as much about Judaism as I could. Maybe doing those things and learning about them would help me understand them. Hey, I thought, it was only going to be for six months. If I didn't like it, I would stop. Besides, if I was ever going to try this, it wasn't going to be any easier than trying it in Jerusalem.

Chapter 1

A "Role" for Women

The debate on what a woman's role should be has ultimately boiled down to the question, Why do women need a "role"? Why should women be pigeonholed into a one-size-fits-all lifestyle that doesn't quite fit anybody?

God does not demand that we fit ourselves into some mold. He endowed us with great power and gave us the Torah to guide us in how to use it properly. The Torah helps us recognize our power and provides us a way to harness it for good and not evil. It does this by giving us a structure for living. This structure does not constrict us. Rather, it provides us a method to be ourselves at our best.

Power means that one can control things according to one's own will. However, it doesn't grant its owner the right to do whatever one wants. Say a worker at ABC corporation was just given much more clout by being made an executive VP. This does not mean that she can do as she pleases with impunity. Rather, the authority she was given is an opportunity for her to benefit the company. Likewise, when God gives a person power, He is giving her an opportunity to improve the world. She will ultimately have to report to Him on how she utilized this opportunity.

Power comes with a commensurate amount of responsibility. Each person has the ability to create and destroy worlds. One's actions affect not only the physical but also the spiritual world. It is one's responsibility to learn the extent of her power and how to wield it wisely. If one fails to do so, she is held accountable for the resulting damage. For example, say a woman sees a person begging for food. Even if the beggar does not look like he's starving, he may be malnourished and sick. The woman has the capability to help the beggar, even if only partially. Her actions may result in saving his life. If she pretends that she doesn't see him then she is denying her power and will be held responsible for the suffering which she could have alleviated.

Once power is recognized and responsibility is accepted, it can be used to attain a goal. Judaism sets the same goal for women and men: to serve God. The Torah provides people with a structure for living to help them meet this objective. These structures are what the roles are. The Torah understands and appreciates the differences between men and women and tailors this structure to their specific needs.

This is analogous to a fitness expert designing workout programs for members of the gym. All programs are engineered using the same principles, and with the same goal in mind: to be physically fit. However, in order to help men and women develop to their full potential, their workout programs must take into account their physiological differences. For example, since men tend to suffer more from cardiac arrest, their routine may emphasize aerobic exercise to decrease cholesterol. Since women suffer more from brittle bones after menopause, their routine may stress weight training, which increases bone density. Note that what is emphasized is not what is ordinarily done. Men usually do not do a lot of aerobics, and many women shy away from weight training.

At the same time, God made each human being a unique individual and not a generic male or female. Therefore, the role given to a person allows room for self-expression. Each person is not only allowed but obligated to use his or her unique talents to serve God. Roles do not inhibit this; they only channel it in a positive manner.

What about having the freedom to do what one wants with one's power? Here we find the key to the Jewish concept of freedom.

Power grants one freedom of choice. However, freedom of choice does not grant freedom, it only makes it an option. In other words, being free does not mean being able to do whatever one wants. It means overcoming one's *yetzer hara*, evil inclination, and doing what is right.

Consider a woman who decides that she wants to be as healthy as possible. She begins with a trip to the gym. The fitness expert shows her the myriad of machines and in great detail explains precisely when, why, and how to do each exercise. To perform these exercises, one needs to follow the rules of each one with concentration and discipline. If she were to "free" herself from these rules then she would at best not get the maximum benefit from the exercise and at worst damage her body for life. It is precisely by following the rules that freedom is attained.

Judaism provides us, men and women, with a gymnasium for the soul. It has its own numerous sets of "exercises" that must be done in a very specific way. Their purpose is not to burden a person, but rather to give her a structure that, if meticulously adhered to, allows her to get the best out of life. In this way, she will attain true freedom.

Chapter 2

Let's Start at the Very Beginning

Personal Reflections

I decided to give Orthodox Judaism one last try out of a sense of intellectual integrity. My biggest problems were all those unanswered questions I had. I put these questions to the Orthodox people at the kosher dining hall in college, but I didn't get any satisfactory answers. I was going to try to find the answers one last time so I could honestly say that I wasn't Orthodox because I didn't believe it was right, not because I did not understand it.

One of the extracurricular activities at Hebrew University was a series of lectures on a variety of topics that was sponsored by an Orthodox group. Since almost all of my most urgent questions had to do with the position of women in Judaism, I went to the lectures on that topic. The lecturer was Gila Manolson and she was amazing. Later I learned that she graduated Yale magna cum laude in music. She later traveled to Israel where she "accidentally" stumbled upon Judaism. She ended up studying in a women's yeshivah in Jerusalem and became one of the lecturers at an outreach organization, Aish HaTorah. What she said opened my mind. There was so much I did not know and I finally found a place where I could learn.

She talked about how Woman was created and the different natures of men and women. The woman was not a subset of a man nor an appendage but an equal and a complement. It struck me that what she said about men and women was so true. Psychologists are learning about the differences only now and Judaism had known about them all along.

A couple of years later, after I had been religious for some time, I chanced upon a book by Rabbi Aryeh Kaplan called *Inner Space*. I had already read another book he wrote, *Waters of Eden*, and was astounded with what clarity he wrote on deep and complex concepts. Whatever the book was about, I was sure it was fascinating. So I bought it. "Fascinating" does not even begin to describe it. It was like the Rosetta stone I was looking for. There were many things that were constantly referenced to in Jewish literature, such as the *sefirot*, which were never fully explained. This book explained many of the terms and concepts that underlie Jewish thought. It also talked a lot about the masculine and feminine aspects of Creation. It made me appreciate just how vital my own role was as a woman.

It Is Not Good for Adam to Be Alone

In the beginning God created Adam. "God created Adam in His image. In the image of God He created him. Male and female created He them."[1] Looking at the switch from the singular "him [Adam]" to the plural "them [male and female]," our Sages understood that originally there was a single Adam who was then split into a male and a female.[2] This teaches us that a male and a female are each only half a person. God originally created a human of both genders so that Adam and Eve and all of their descendants would have a memory, at least on some primordial level, of that ultimate level of completeness.[3] This is why people who are single often feel that there is something missing in their lives. Only when uniting in marriage do they become whole again.

If Adam was originally complete, why did God then divide this being into two incomplete people? "God said, 'It is not good for Adam to be alone.' "[4] Even though Adam was complete, he was alone. At this point God led all the animals in front of Adam for him to name.[5] Naming something in Hebrew means more than assigning vocal expressions to refer to it. Hebrew letters are like the table of chemical elements but in the spiritual realm. Each one represents an elemental spiritual force. A Hebrew name therefore describes the essence of the thing. It is like the name H_2O for water. When Adam named all the animals, he thereby perceived their essence. Having seen and understood all the other creatures, Adam was able to fully appreciate that there was no equal companion for him. He felt truly alone.

One of the most direct ways of connecting to God is by imitating Him. The main method of imitating God is by giving.

---

1 Genesis 1:27.
2 *Eruvin* 18a.
3 *Zohar, Tazria* 43b.
4 Genesis 2:18.
5 Ibid., 19–20.

Giving requires one to loosen one's self-centered view of the world and to concentrate on another person's needs. The more one gives, the more attuned one becomes to others. This expands one's world beyond one's self to include another person, then a group of people, then a community, then all of human-kind.

Giving teaches a person about God, the ultimate and constant Giver, and helps her appreciate God's gifts to her. It is like a daughter not being able to appreciate all her mother has done for her until she becomes a mother herself. Giving also allows a person to become an agent of God. She will not only be blessed, but she can now also be a blessing to others.

By being complete, Adam's opportunity to give was very limited. By separating the male and female, God created two halves who deeply needed each other. Only by constant giving of one's self could total unity now be achieved. Adam and Eve would now be able to imitate God. Not surprisingly, giving and loving are closely related. The root of the word love, *ahavah*, is *hav*, which means to give.[1] The constant opportunities to give of one's self is what makes marriage such a powerful vehicle for growth, love, and holiness.

I Will Make Him an Ezer K'negdo

As soon as Adam realized how alone he was, God put him in a deep sleep and proceeded to build what He called an "*ezer k'negdo.*"[2] An *ezer* is a helper. Some have reasoned that because a woman is described as a helper and was created after a man, she

---

1   Compare Psalms 29 to Genesis 29:21.
2   Genesis 2:18.

is inferior to the man and a mere supplement to him. For one thing, as we have seen it is not really true that a woman was created after a man. Furthermore, a person can be helped by a servant, a colleague, or God. Being a helper is no indication of one's relative status.

Since animals were created before humankind, one could argue that a man should be considered inferior to a cockroach. For some reason, I have never heard this "proof" of a woman's inferiority applied to a man.

The purpose of Creation was to be a vehicle through which God could give the greatest good. This "greatest good" is God himself. In order for God to give, there must be a proper receiver. However, if the receiver only receives, then it becomes the antithesis of God, who is a giver. Therefore, a creature had to be created which could receive from God, transform it into a gift for God, and then give this gift back to God.[1]

God created the world using ten "building blocks" called *sefirot* (*sefirah* in the singular) or "emanations." The first three *sefirot* describe the process by which the world was built. The next six describe different forms of giving. The tenth *sefirah*, *Malchut*, describes the process by which one receives the seeds from the preceding six giving *sefirot*, unifies these seeds into one unit, allows this unit to gestate and develop, and gives back the finished product. The physical model that represents *Malchut* is the womb.[2] While the "giving" *sefirot* are male, *Malchut* is female.

Creation progressed from the emanation of the "giving" *sefirot*, the male aspect of Creation, to the emanation of *Malchut*,

---

1 Aryeh Kaplan, *Inner Space* (Jerusalem: Moznaim Publishing Corporation, 1991), 75–76.
2 Ibid.

the female aspect of Creation. Adam's role vis-à-vis the rest of Creation was to use it in the worship of God. Creation was to provide the seeds and Adam was the "womb." This is why Adam was created last. While Adam had both a male and female aspect to him, it was the male aspect which had consciousness first. This is why Adam is referred to in male terms even before the split. The female part was made into a separate, independent being after the creation of Adam because she was the "womb" of Adam.

To make sure there are no misinterpretations, let us emphasize that in this context, the "womb" refers to the whole concept of *Malchut*. Therefore, the woman being referred to as the "womb" of Adam is not meant to imply that she is nothing more than a uterus. The woman was never seen as being just a baby machine. This is reflected in Jewish law, where the woman is not obligated to bear children.

What kind of a helper is an *"ezer k'negdo"*? *K'negdo* can mean "opposite," as in standing opposite to someone. When the woman was brought to the man, she was facing him. In this way, she could see things he could not, and she had a different perspective on the things that they both saw. Therefore, one way a woman can help a man is by using her own perspective.

Another meaning of *k'negdo* is "against." There are times when a woman must oppose her husband in order to help him. The purpose of a true helper is to aid someone to reach the highest spiritual heights he can. A woman cannot do this by simply being an accomplice. She must encourage and advise, and she must also actively oppose when the situation warrants. Another interpretation is that if a man is worthy, the woman will be his helper. If he is not worthy, she will be against him.[1]

What about the woman? Who helps her reach her spiritual

1 *Yevamot* 63a.

heights? What does she get out of helping the man? What does the man do for her? Is she supposed to just constantly give without receiving anything in return? Does she have an individual identity or independent purpose?

The woman is rewarded for being an *ezer k'negdo* on many levels. On the most practical level, she makes the man a better person. Through her influence, he becomes a better husband, a better father, and a better member of the community. This leads to a happier marriage and family, and a stronger community. In addition to the reward one gets for helping others, being an *ezer k'negdo* allows a woman to fulfill a unique aspect of her spiritual potential. This will be discussed later.

One must keep in mind that this relationship of the woman to the man does not mean that help can only go one way. Certainly the man helps the woman become a better person as well. Through encouragement, constructive criticism, and by example, the man and woman can equally help each other improve his or her character traits.

But these are scanty, simple answers that don't get to the heart of the questions. Neither do they answer the fundamental question: Why is the woman an *ezer k'negdo* to the man? (Why isn't the man an *ezer k'negdo* to the woman? Why can't both be an *ezer k'negdo* to each other?)

The Giver/Initiator and the Receiver/Completer

In the Jewish male-female archetype, the male is the Giver/Initiator, represented by the six *sefirot* of giving, and the female is the Receiver/Completer, that is, *Malchut*.[1] The male be-

---

1   Kaplan, *Inner Space*, 42.

gins a process by giving the raw materials to the female. The female then receives these materials from the male and transforms them into a product which is of a much higher order of complexity and holiness.

Keep in mind that these male-female archetypes are not meant to fully describe men and women, but male and female characteristics. Men and women have both male and female characteristics. Male characteristics are generally dominant with men, and female characteristics are generally dominant with women.

A prime example of the Giver-Receiver dynamic is the creation of new life. A male gives the female a single sperm cell. The female receives it, holds it in her womb, and uses her feminine strength to produce a human being. Note that a woman provides her own seed as well, illustrating that men and women are much more complex than the archetypes we are discussing, since they have both masculine and feminine characteristics. Traditionally, the man as the main income earner would bring money home to the woman. She would convert the money into the building of a home and the performance of mitzvot such as welcoming guests and giving to the needy.

The Talmud states this point as follows: "How does a woman help a man? ... If a man brings wheat, does he chew the wheat? If flax, does he put on the flax? Does she not then bring light to his eyes and put him on his feet?" These are meant as rhetorical questions which are to be understood beyond their face value. The man brings the woman the raw material, for example wheat or flax. These are useless by themselves. The man needs the woman to grind the wheat and make bread and to spin the flax to make linen. That is, he needs her to actualize the potential of his contributions.

We can use this archetype to understand many of the gender references in Judaism. God is generally referred to in male terms, even though He has no gender. There is absolutely nothing we can say about *who* God is. This is simply beyond human understanding. The only things we can talk about is what He does and the relationship we have with Him.[1]

We are always praying to God to give us things, be they health, wisdom, peace, or a comfortable livelihood. The Hebrew word for "to pray" is *l'hitpallel*, which is a self-reflexive verb that also means "to judge oneself." Praying is therefore not about presenting a laundry list of needs and wants to God. It is about first looking within and examining what one needs in order to improve one's service to God, and only then praying for it. For example, it is not enough to just ask God for more money. Praying requires that one first examine if one really needs the extra money, and how that money will be used to perform God's will. Perhaps a more comfortable livelihood would allow one to devote more time to study Torah and do good deeds. With this purpose in mind, one can then approach God and pray. In praying, we are thereby asking God to give us the raw materials we need (hence the male appellation) so that we can raise ourselves to a higher level.

The relationship between God and Israel is often described as that between husband and wife. God gave Israel the Torah. Using the Torah, Israel can now prepare this physical world for a holier level of existence. She does this by keeping the commandments, thereby making the world a vessel where holiness can be contained.

Then the relationship between God and Israel is switched, and we refer to God in the feminine as the *Shechinah*, the divine

1   Ibid., 9.

34

presence. Israel has labored in the Torah and prepared the vessels. Israel, now as the male, presents his work and the *Shechinah* comes and fills these vessels with holiness. When the Jews were in the desert, God commanded them to build a sanctuary so that He could dwell within (among) them. The Jews built the sanctuary to God's exact specifications and the *Shechinah* dwelled among the people. The divine presence was so strong that it was tangible. It resided as a cloud over the sanctuary and later in the Temples.

This drama between God and Israel is played out every week, culminating on Shabbat. Keeping Shabbat has two aspects to it: remembering and observing. As the Torah says, "Remember [*zachor*] the Sabbath day to sanctify it. Six days shall you work and accomplish all your work."[1] We are also commanded, "The Children of Israel shall observe [*shamor*] the Sabbath, to make the Sabbath an eternal covenant for their generations."[2] The command to work the other six days follows immediately after we are told to remember the Shabbat. One interpretation of this is that remembering Shabbat means that one should prepare for it every day during the rest of the week.[3] Note that *zachor*, remember, has the same root as *zachar*, which means male. During the week, Israel labors as the male, preparing the raw materials, such as the festive meals, in order to observe (*shamor*) the Shabbat. While the six days of the week are considered masculine, "Shabbat" is feminine. It receives Israel's raw materials and transports Israel to a holier dimension of living.

We experience the Shabbat in three stages. On Friday night,

---

1 Exodus 20:8–9.
2 Ibid. 31:16.
3 Rabbi Nosson Scherman, and Rabbi Meir Zlotowitz, ed., *The Chumash* (New York: Mesorah Publications, Ltd., 1996), 410. See comment to Exodus 20:8.

we experience God as a Queen. We welcome the *Shechinah*, a most honored guest in our homes. On Saturday morning, we experience God as a King. During the morning prayer services, we read from the Torah and hear God's commandments to us. The cycle is about to begin again. But before we begin climbing another rung on the spiral, we are given a taste of what it is we are climbing to. The theme of Shabbat afternoon is the coming of the Messiah, the Redemption, and the World to Come — a state of completion and perfection. This is when the King and Queen now unite in Oneness. We appreciate how wonderful this world is on Shabbat, and look forward to the time when the world will be like this all the time. Our partnership with God has come full circle, but now we are on a higher level of the cycle. We have ascended a rung in a spiral.

Why a Woman Is an Ezer K'negdo to the Man

In Genesis it is written, "And God blessed the seventh day and made it holy, because on it [He] rested from all the work that He had done to do."[1] The seemingly superfluous "to do" at the end tells us that creation was not finished. God had left a part of it unfinished for the purpose of letting Man finish it.[2] Man is then able to be a helper to God. Certainly God does not need Man's help. But being a helper to God is an excellent educational tool to Man. It is like a mother giving her three-year-old son the challah to bring to the table. The mother could have just as easily done it herself. However, letting the child "help" her teaches him a lot about honoring one's parents and doing acts of

---

1 Genesis 2:3.
2 *Radak* on Genesis 2:3.

chesed (kindness), and it is a great self-esteem builder.

Man was created as a transitional creature between the physical and spiritual worlds. By giving him a physical and spiritual side as well as free will, God made it possible for Man to utilize the physical for spiritual ends. Man can now elevate the physical to the spiritual level, and make it possible for the world to be filled with God's holiness. In this way, Man acts as a helper to God and completes His work, thereby fulfilling the ultimate goal of Creation.

Turnus Rufus[1] once taunted Rabbi Akiva, the great second century scholar and teacher, that the mitzvah of circumcision is evidence that God created man as an imperfect creature. Rabbi Akiva agreed, saying, "The handiwork of man is more pleasant than that of the Holy One." In order to prove his point, Rabbi Akiva placed a sack of wheat (the handiwork of God) and a row of pastries (the handiwork of man) before Turnus Rufus and asked him which he preferred.[2]

We can now answer our earlier questions. Mankind is a helper to God because he completes God's work: transforming the raw materials into the finished products. Likewise, a woman is a helper to the man because of her unique ability to complete his work. This is why Man is considered the crown of creation, and the woman is considered the crown of her husband. The crown is symbolic of having attained a higher status.

There are two ways to provide help: by providing the seed, and by providing the channel. When one provides the seed, one gives someone the raw materials for him to develop. Examples of this type of helper are a teacher or a parent who provide the

---

1 Roman governor of Judea during the first century C.E. who destroyed the Second Temple.
2 *Midrash Tanchuma, Tazria* 5.

seeds for the child's moral, emotional, intellectual, and spiritual development.

When one provides the channel, then one is using his unique capabilities to completely actualize the seed's potential. An example of this is the student who internalizes his teachings and uses them to grow and develop.

The husband and wife give each other both types of help. The one that comes most naturally is when the husband is the giver/initiator and the wife is the receiver/completer. However, when a wife gives her husband advice and encouragement, or when she opposes him, then she is being a giver. It is up to the husband to take her seeds of wisdom and bring them to fruition by becoming a better person. This type of help goes contrary to the woman's and the man's nature. The woman is generally reluctant to say something disagreeable to her husband, especially when it would upset him or start a fight. The husband does not like to be told what he should or shouldn't do.

The Torah often emphasizes that which is least natural. For example, it commands one to love God,[1] the convert,[2] and one's fellow Jew.[3] Nowhere does it say that one must love one's parents, one's spouse, or one's children. Why does the Torah not command us to love the most important people in our lives? One reason may be because it comes naturally. Instead, God chose to emphasize that which requires great effort.

Another example is that we are required to mourn twelve months when a parent dies and thirty days when any other member of the immediate family dies. Since it is natural to bury one's parents and unnatural to bury, for example, a child, one

---

1   Deuteronomy 6:5.
2   Leviticus 19:34.
3   Ibid., 18.

might rationalize mourning less for a parent since this is a normal life event. Therefore, the Torah needs to emphasize the need to mourn for the parent. When one buries a child, the Torah need not emphasize the mourning since that pain is now indelible to the mourning parent.

Even though the term *ezer* refers to the woman, it is in the male form, thereby alluding to the male form of help. Therefore, even though both a husband and wife help each other, the Torah emphasizes the type of help that is the most difficult for a woman to give and a man to receive.

Through the dynamic of the male-female relationship, the man and woman are able to express themselves and fulfill their spiritual potential. The couple becomes partners with God in creation and sanctification.

Sarah: A Model of Being an Ezer K'negdo

In practice, there are as many ways of being an *ezer k'negdo* as there are women. Here we will look at just one example of how Sarah, our Matriarch, was able to guide her husband and save the future of Israel.

Sarah was a partner with her husband, Abraham, in teaching the world about God. Abraham taught the men while Sarah taught the women.[1] Here we see one way that Sarah acted as an *ezer k'negdo* — by working in a partnership with her husband.

Another way Sarah was an *ezer k'negdo* was by creating a holy home. She was one of the greatest prophetesses. The sanctuary in the desert and later the Temple are actually modeled after her home. Sarah was a holy person, and she imbued all her

---

1 *Bereishit Rabbah* on Genesis 12:18.

activities and surroundings with holiness. As a testament to what went on inside, God made His presence felt by placing His cloud of holiness over Sarah's tent. This same cloud rested on the Mishkan, the sanctuary in the desert, and later the Temple.[1]

Sarah and Abraham were childless, yet they knew that somehow the nation of Israel would be born from Abraham (it was not yet revealed that Sarah was to be the mother).[2] As an act of immense personal sacrifice, Sarah decided to give her Egyptian maidservant, Hagar, as a wife to Abraham. In this way she was hoping to raise the child Hagar would give birth to so that both she and Abraham would have progeny.[3] Hagar conceived immediately and began to act in a haughty manner to Sarah. She even began to view Sarah's righteousness as suspect.[4] When Sarah tried to put Hagar in her place, Hagar ran away.

When Hagar was by a spring of water in the desert, an angel appeared to her and told her to go back to her mistress. He also promised her that she would have a lot of offspring. When she would return, she would conceive again (she had miscarried) and bear a son whom she should name Ishmael.[5] Ishmael would be "a wild-ass of a man; his hand against everyone, and everyone's hand against him."[6] And so it was.

Thirteen years later, God came to Abraham and revealed, among other things, that he was going to have a son with Sarah (who was already eighty-nine years old!), his son's name was to be Isaac, and it would be through him that God's covenant with

---

1   ArtScroll Tanach Series, *Bereishis*, vol. 3 (New York: Mesorah Publications, Ltd., 1978), 837.

2   Genesis 16:1.

3   Ibid., 2.

4   Ibid., 4; see Rashi's comment.

5   Ibid., 6–11.

6   Ibid., 12.

Abraham would be maintained. "But I will maintain My covenant through Isaac, whom Sarah will bear to you by this time next year."[1] Note that the text does not just say "But I will maintain My covenant through Isaac," which would have been enough to convey the same information since we already knew that Sarah was to bear him. However, there are no extra words in the Torah. If something seems superfluous, that means that it is there to teach us something. By saying "Isaac, whom Sarah will bear to you," the Torah emphasizes Sarah's role in shaping the second Patriarch of Israel.

When Isaac was a child, Sarah saw Ishmael "mock" Isaac.[2] This was no ordinary childish mockery. The term used in the Torah is *mitzachek*, which is also used in Scripture to denote the three cardinal sins: idolatry,[3] adultery,[4] and murder.[5] Therefore, Ishmael's behavior demonstrated that he was thoroughly corrupt and evil.[6] Sarah acted immediately. She told Abraham to kick out Hagar and her son. Even though Sarah had hoped to raise the child, he was obviously completely under Hagar's influence and so was called by her name.

While it greatly distressed Abraham to see that Ishmael had fallen to evil ways, he did not want to evict him and his mother. "So God said to Abraham, 'Be not distressed over the youth or your maidservant: Whatever Sarah tells you, heed her voice, since through Isaac will offspring be considered yours.' "[7] God did not just tell Abraham to evict Hagar and Ishmael, nor did He

---

1   Ibid. 17:21.
2   Ibid. 21:9.
3   Exodus 32:6.
4   Ibid. 39:17.
5   II Samuel 2:14.
6   Genesis 21:9; see Rashi's comment.
7   Ibid., 12.

say that in this case Sarah was right. Instead, God made a more general statement, "Whatever Sarah tells you, heed her voice." Had Ishmael remained, he would have had a corrupting influence on Isaac, and ultimately all of Israel. By demanding that he be removed from the house swiftly, Sarah acted as an *ezer k'negdo* to help her husband fulfill the covenant with God, and in her capacity as a matriarch to ensure the welfare of her children.

Differences between Men and Women

Justifications for Suspicion

Women are often very suspicious at even the hint that men and women are different. In the past, men and women were not simply considered different from each other. The man was the human being, the ideal, and the norm. Any difference observed in the woman, whether due to nature or nurture, was therefore seen as a deviation from the norm and less than ideal. No one ever considered that a woman was nothing more or less than human. A different human than a man, but a human nonetheless.

The first challenge for feminists was (and sometimes still is) to show that a woman is a human being. Since the only model of being truly "human" was to be a man, feminists called for women being as much like men as possible. The ideal liberated woman was one who concentrated on her career in a male-dominated field at the expense of her personal life. The goal was to break into exclusive male enclaves of money and power, break through the glass ceiling, and get to the top. The real challenge was to prove to men, to women, and especially to oneself, that women were just as capable as men.

Women have made great progress in changing people's attitudes about what women are able to do. There is no longer any serious doubt among most men and women of women's abilities and talents. This has caused views of women as being the Weaker Sex to become outdated. Women's success gave them a measure of self-esteem, a sense of accomplishment, self-confidence, and independence. It made women more secure about their place in society.

If the first question that was answered was "Can I do this?" then the next question that women are now asking is "What do I want to do?" This is quite a radical question. It assumes that a woman might have different goals than a man, that this is okay, and that a woman must actively choose the path to her own happiness.

As women are reaching critical mass in the social sciences, such as psychology, they are becoming active participants in debating theories on differences between men and women. In the past, theories on differences were inseparable from theories of women's inferiority, and so for a feminist to admit a difference would have been tantamount to admitting a weakness. Now women are approaching this discussion from a position of strength, and it is now possible to consider that women may be different without being inferior.

One assumption that is being questioned is that equality between the sexes means making the woman equal to the man. The problem is that the man is still considered the standard by which women should be treated. The underlying rationale is that women are or could be, and they definitely should be, just like men. One does not even need to believe that men and women differ by nature in order to realize the fallacy of this thinking. As Carol Tavris points out in her book, *The Mismeasure of Woman*,

> As in medicine, the law regards the male as the legal standard of a human being. Therefore, women may be treated like men, in which case they are equal to them, or not like men, in which case they are deficient or special. But they are never treated specifically as women.[1]

This attitude is apparent in such well-meaning questions as: Why aren't girls taking as many math and science classes as boys? Why aren't they majoring as much in engineering as boys? Why aren't there as many female CEO's in the Fortune 500 as male? In other words, why aren't women doing what men are doing? One valid reason is discrimination. Girls are told that they aren't good in math and science. They get subtle and not-so-subtle hints that they are not as smart as boys. They do not have as many role models as boys. Boys are told that they are superior to girls.

But if discrimination is the only reason for the discrepancies, then we are left with the assumption that, all else being equal, women could and should be just like men. Now let's ask some other questions: Why are boys not majoring in psychology as much as girls? Why do they not take care of children as much? Why are they so obsessed with their careers at the expense of their personal life? In other words, why are boys not acting more like girls? The answer is, who wants to act like a girl? We must be careful not to take the view that whatever boys do is entirely good and beyond reproach, while the girls are the ones with all the problems.

---

1 Carol Tavris, *The Mismeasure of Woman* (New York: Simon and Schuster, 1992), 106.

Women are also questioning the whole method by which they are evaluated and compared to men. Carol Gilligan, in her landmark book, *In a Different Voice*, writes how the theories of human development in modern psychology are based on research done by men on other men.[1] Women were footnoted as being different and not fitting the model, and that is the extent to which their experiences were considered. Furthermore, the theories still assume the "human" is a man, while women are given auxiliary roles in the "human's" development. Women are not themselves included in this process of maturation.

In order to talk meaningfully about men and women, one must first reject man as the standard by which woman is judged. This means rejecting the view that what was considered masculine in traditional American society is automatically superior, and what was considered feminine is inferior. One also needs to have a healthy respect for oneself and for men, and realize that we all have our respective strengths and weaknesses.

Differences Between Men and Women

God created the world using three mental faculties — that is, three ways of knowing: *chochmah*, *binah*, and *daat*. These are the first three *sefirot* mentioned earlier. When you rearrange the letters of *chochmah*, you get the words *koach mah*, "the potential of what."[2] *Chochmah* is the answer to the question "What?" What is it? What happens? For example, what color is your shirt? Red. What do the stars seem to do at night? They move across the sky. *Chochmah* represents the axioms, the givens, the observations. *Chochmah* lies outside of logic. For example, one cannot prove

---

1   Carol Gilligan, *In a Different Voice: Psychological Theory and Women's Development* (Cambridge: Harvard Press, 1993), 9–13.

2   Kaplan, *Inner Space*, 58.

45

that something is red. Either she sees it or she does not or she relies on someone else's vision. If one were an astronomer in ancient times, she would not prove that stars move across the Earth's sky. She would proceed to figure out how they do this. Either one accepts an axiom or she rejects it, either she knows it or she does not. Men and women are considered as having equal measures of *chochmah*.

In order to build a woman, God took out a "*tzela*" from Adam.[1] A "*tzela*" means a "side," so a woman came from a side of Adam. The nature of which side she came from can be understood from the other meaning of "*tzela*," which is a rib. A rib is internal and it protects the viscera, the vital organs on which survival depends.

After God took out a *tzela*, He "built" a woman.[2] The root of the word for "to build" is *banah*, which is related to the word for understanding, *binah*. From this the sages learned that women have a greater measure of *binah*.[3] *Binah* is defined as understanding something from something dissimilar.[4] It also has the same root as *bein*, which means "between." These two explanations combined teach us that *binah* is the ability to learn something from something dissimilar due to one's ability to discern a connection. Knowledge is seen as a web. *Binah* also implies a connection between the person and the subject. In psychology, this is called "connected knowing," which has been recognized as dominant in women.

As Belenky, et al., write in *Women's Ways of Knowing*,

Connected Knowers develop procedures for gaining

---

1   Genesis 2:21.
2   Ibid., 22.
3   *Niddah* 45b.
4   *Sanhedrin* 93b.

access to other people's knowledge. At the heart of these procedures is the capacity for empathy. Since knowledge comes from experience, the only way they can hope to understand another person's ideas is to try to share the experience that has led the person to form the idea.... But insofar as possible, they must act as connected rather than separate selves, seeing the other not in their own terms but in the other's terms.[1]

When a Connected Knower asks, "Why do you think that?" she does not mean, "What were the steps in your reasoning?" but "What circumstances led you to that perception?"[2]

It has long been known in Western culture that women think differently than men. Only recently has research been done on how exactly women think with the attitude that "women's ways of knowing" are just as important and relevant as men's. This is something which has always been a part of Judaism.

Men have a greater measure of *daat. Daat* is when one understands something by first separating one's ego from the subject. In psychology, this is called "separate knowing," which has been recognized as dominant in men.

> Separate knower's procedures for making meaning are strictly impersonal. Feelings and personal beliefs are rigorously excluded.... Separate knowers try to "weed out the self" so that the flowers of pure reason may flourish.[3]

The crucial difference between separate knowing as de-

---

1 Mary Field Belenky, et al., *Women's Ways of Knowing: The Development of Self, Voice, and Mind* (USA: Basic Books, Inc., 1986), 113.
2 Ibid., 114.
3 Ibid., 109

scribed in modern psychology and *daat* is how the subject is viewed. As an example, let us use a moral dilemma as the subject. For people who are not religious, who are the vast majority of research subjects in modern psychology, solving a moral dilemma has as much significance as solving any other civic or personal problem. For people who are religious, everything is viewed as coming from God, and any question becomes a quest for learning how to better live in accordance with God's will. Also, the wrong moral decision is seen as having eternal consequences in this world and in the world to come. With this perspective, any subject of inquiry is viewed with love and reverence. The very goal of the inquiry is to connect with God by understanding a particular question. Separate knowing becomes a means to an end, but is not viewed as the end in itself.

By themselves, both separate knowing and connected knowing lead to problems. With connected knowing, there is a lot of personal involvement with the subject. The goal is to understand things from the subject's point of view, and it is thus necessary to refrain from imposing one's own viewpoint. The risk is loss of objectivity and the crumbling of one's sense of morality under the weight of relativism.[1] With separate knowing there is the risk of being impersonal, indifferent, and blinded to reality by the glare of abstract principles.[2] This can be demonstrated in the field of medicine where the overemphasis on separate knowing and objectivity has made doctors forget that they are treating people, not diseases.

These differences between men and women are apparent in every fiber of their being. One area is how they view themselves and others. Women view themselves in relation to others and

---

1 Gilligan, *In a Different Voice,* 79–89.
2 Ibid., 100.

the world in general. Being mothers, wives, daughters, girl-friends, and friends are a large part of many women's identity. They also view themselves in these roles in a more universal context. For example, in Gilligan's study, a woman aspiring to be a scientist describes herself as "maternal" and how through science she hopes to take care of the world.[1] Men talk about themselves in more abstract ways, and as separate from others. Their careers and achievements are central to their self-definition. Relations to others are usually described in vague terms, if at all.[2]

The danger for a man is that he gets himself into a solipsistic cocoon where he becomes incapable of expressing emotions or forging connections with those closest to him. For example, the men who were the epitome of a "healthy" life cycle as modeled by psychologists were distant in their relationships, even with their wives and children. Close friendships were rare.[3] The danger for a woman is that she loses her own identity and lives only for and through others.[4] These two dangers combined result in the absence of the woman's voice from a relationship.[5] The woman becomes so enwrapped in listening to others that she neglects to listen to herself. The man does not realize that she has a voice, or he suppresses it through domination.

Gilligan noted that as men and women mature, they converge in their thinking.[6] Women rediscover their voice, and they use it. Men become more attuned to those around them and

---

1   Ibid., 158–159.
2   Daniel Levinson, *The Seasons of a Man's Life* (New York: Alfred A. Knopf, 1978).
3   Ibid.
4   Gilligan, *In a Different Voice*, xiii.
5   Ibid.
6   Ibid., 157–158.

build relationships. It is as if men and women start at the bottom of a mountain at opposite ends. As they ascend, they become closer to each other in their views.

This story of maturation is found in Genesis. Originally God created Adam who was both male and female. However, the female was completely subsumed in the male. The female had no identity, and as a result the male was alone. As has been shown, this was an important intermediary state. However, God stated that "It is not good, Adam being alone." God then proceeded to separate out the female and give her her own identity and her own perspective. The male was no longer alone but in a relationship. The female was still in a relationship, but had a distinct voice. When God had finished creating the woman, he brought her to the man. The man said, "This one I will call woman [*ishah*] because she was taken from a man [*ish*]."[1] This is the first time in the Torah that the word *man*, not *Adam*, is used. At this point, God was able to finally say that all of Creation was "very good."

Torah: The Perfect Balance

Since Jewish scholarship and philosophy was developed almost exclusively by men, one would expect Judaism to be structured in the same way as all other male-dominated institutions. One would expect to see strict hierarchical structures with an emphasis on reason and separation and a devaluation of feeling and attachment. Yet this is not the case.

First we will examine how Jews view God by looking at the first words of every blessing, "Blessed are You, God, our Lord, King of the Universe, who has sanctified us with His mitzvot,

---

1 Genesis 2:23.

and has commanded us...." The very first word is "blessed," *baruch*. When we talk about God being blessed, we are referring to His being the source of all blessing. The word *baruch* has the same root as the word *bereichah*, a spring of water, which is a feminine word. The first thing we say about God is that He is like a spring of water, gushing with blessings for His creation. This assumes that He is quite intimately attached to His creation and is occupied with nurturing it.

The next word is "You." We are addressing God not through messengers or intermediaries, but directly! The following word is the tetragrammaton, the four-lettered ineffable name of God, "YHVH." Every name of God refers to a different aspect of our relationship to Him. This name actually underscores our inadequacy in understanding God. The letters of this name can be arranged to spell "was," "is," and "will be." That is, God exists outside of time — it was He who created time. Who He is is entirely beyond human understanding. He is completely Other and Unknowable. He is wholly independent of Creation. And yet, this name contains the recipe for Charity — the way in which God creates and interacts with His creation. This topic is beyond the scope of this book. It is covered with great clarity in Rabbi Aryeh Kaplan's book, *Inner Space*.

The next three words are *Elokeinu melech ha'olam*, "our Lord, King of the Universe." In the beginning of the blessing, we emphasize God's intimate relationship to us, akin to a loving parent. We then say that He is completely independent of us and beyond our understanding. Now we reaffirm our relationship. But now we acknowledge a different type of relationship — that of King and subject. He is both a loving parent and a King. Our relationship to Him is filled with both intimacy and reverence.

The remainder of the blessing is "who has sanctified us

with His mitzvot, and has commanded us [to perform the particular commandment]." Our relationship to God as a King is in many ways opposite from our relationship to a human king. A human king wants people to obey him for his own benefit. The lower the people degrade themselves in his service, the more grandiose he is. God, however, wants to sanctify us. It is we who are elevated by our service to God; God Himself remains the same no matter what we do. God told us in very explicit terms exactly how we are to sanctify ourselves — by performing His commandments! One reason He gave us so many commandments was to provide us with many opportunities for elevating ourselves. This was all done for our own benefit, not His.

The language of blessings shows us that our relationship with God requires both connection and separation, intimacy and hierarchy. It is through this balance of masculine and feminine ways of understanding that a complete picture emerges.

Next, we will look at how men and women view morality according to current research and contrast that with how Judaism views morality. When asked what morality meant to them, men expressed strong beliefs in abstract principles of right and wrong.[1] They stressed not having their rights violated and not violating others' rights.[2] As the men matured, they became more sensitive to the rights of others.[3] Women believed that morality was relative and depended on the person and the situation.[4] They equated morality with obligations and responsibilities to others.[5] Of paramount importance was not hurting others.[6] As

---

1 Ibid.

2 Lawrence Kohlberg, *The Philosophy of Moral Development* (San Francisco: Harper and Row, 1981).

3 J. M. Murphy and C. Gilligan, "Moral Development in Late Adolescence and Adulthood: A Critique and Reconstruction of Kohlberg's Theory," *Human Development* 23 (1980), 77–104.

they matured they included the need to take care of themselves as well in their definition of morality.[1]

In Judaism, morality means observing God's commandments as described in the Torah. This implies a set of absolute principles of what is right and wrong which are Truth. At the same time, Jewish law is not monolithic — it does not have simple answers to every question. When Moses was on Mount Sinai, God gave him not only the written Torah, the Five Books of Moses, but also an oral tradition, which later was written down and called the Talmud. It is the Talmud which teaches us how to observe the commandments and how to apply the principles of the Torah to every day life.

In most areas of Jewish law, there is much disagreement between the greatest sages as to how these principles are to be applied. All these opinions are valid because they are arrived at through an accepted process of Talmudic (legal) reasoning. In studying the Talmud, the goal is not to arrive at neat answers. Very few final answers are given. Rather, the goal is to learn how to construct arguments. The Torah was not meant to be "in Heaven" — a set of abstract principles from on high. It is called a Living Torah — it is meant to be applied to daily living and take into account all its complexity. The Torah itself teaches us how to do this.

Commandments can be divided into two types: those between a person and God and those between a person and another person. The commandments that are between people spell out each person's responsibilities to others. For example, we are com-

---

4   Ibid., 102.

5   Gilligan, *In a Different Voice*, 65.

6   Ibid., 102–103.

1   Ibid., 157–158.

manded to take care of the poor, the orphan, the widow, the stranger. We must redeem Jewish captives. Jews are seen as constituting a single body where if even the smallest part of it hurts, then the whole body is in pain. Observing the commandments reinforces the concept of interdependence between the individual and the community.

One is also obligated to take care of oneself. For example, as important as giving charity is, one is not allowed to give so much that he endangers his own welfare. There is also a hierarchy of priorities when obligations conflict. For example, one is obligated to honor and respect his or her parents.[1] Included in this obligation is the prohibition of contradicting them.[2] However, there are limits to how much one must defer one's own needs to those of his or her parents. For example, one may marry the person of one's choice even if his parents object.[3] Also, if one must choose between upsetting one's parents and upsetting one's marital peace, the law is clear that marital peace takes precedence.[4] This is equally true for sons and daughters.[5]

We are responsible not only for others' physical welfare, but also for their spiritual welfare. For example, we must remove stumbling blocks for the blind. This is meant not only for people who are physically blind but also spiritually blind to some matter. We must also rebuke others when we see them doing something wrong.[6] This implies that there is a standard of right and

1 Exodus 20:12.
2 This is considered part of the commandment to revere them (Deuteronomy 5:16).
3 *Rama* 240:25, based on *Maharik* 176.
4 Rambam, *Hilchot Ishut*, 13:14.
5 Ibid.
6 There are a lot of limitations to this commandment to ensure that it is not abused. First, it only applies to sins committed in public. One is prohibited from invading another's privacy to make sure that she is moral. Also, one is

wrong, and an ethic of care and responsibility to others. It is not enough that one is moral; we are all in one boat and if someone makes a hole under his seat then we all sink.

When studying how boys and girls play,[1] researchers have found that boys developed an elaborate system of rules for deciding disputes. Their priority was figuring out what was right. Girls generally ended the game when a dispute arose so as not to endanger the relationship. Their priority was peace. The Talmud is certainly the most elaborate system of rules ever created. Yet in the Torah we are commanded to go beyond the rules whenever possible so as to treat people not just fairly, but nicely. Wherever possible, the judges in a Jewish court of law will encourage the disputants to accept a compromise. Compromise is the way by which a judgment can achieve both Truth and Peace. If both parties give a little and take a little, then they can go out of the courtroom at best as friends, at worst as they were before the dispute, but at least not as enemies.

Feminists have theorized how the legal system would function if it was developed according to "women's ways of knowing." As Steve Friedell demonstrates in his article, "The 'Different Voice' in Jewish Law: Some Parallels to a Feminist Jurisprudence,"[2] the feminist ideal would be very similar to the Jewish le-

---

only obligated to rebuke someone who will listen to the rebuker. If one's words will have no effect, or if they will make the situation worse, then she should not say anything. If possible, she should find someone whom the person will listen to and have him give the rebuke. Finally, the rebuke must be done in a righteous way. Just because a person did something wrong does not give one the right to treat him badly. One may not embarrass the other person or hurt his feelings, or transgress any other commandment concerning how we are to treat people.

1 Janet Lever, "Sex Differences in the Games Children Play," *Social Problems* 23 (1976): 478–487.

2 Steve Friedel, "The 'Different Voice' in Jewish Law: Some Parallels to a Feminist Jurisprudence," *Indiana Law Journal* (Fall 1992): 915–949.

gal system. Both view the goal of the legal process to be peace and not strict, blind justice. The assumption is that both litigants are part of a community where all members are interdependent. Therefore, the ideal manner of solving disputes is one where the relationship between the parties is repaired. The person who would be most suited to be a judge must therefore be not only scholarly but also compassionate and in touch with the community. Lawyers are seen as unnecessary in most cases and impediments to this process. As Friedell states,

> [T]he emphasis of Jewish law on promoting compromise rather than litigation according to strict law was expressly for the reason of promoting peace. The Talmudic rabbis sought to exclude lawyers from the litigation process because it was thought that they would interfere with the peaceful resolution of disputes.... A community was to appoint men of compassion to be judges.... And each member of the community had a duty to look out for the other member's welfare.... [I]t is obvious that a feminist jurisprudence based on Carol Gilligan's approach has much in common with Jewish law.[1]

One possible reason why Judaism was developed in such a balanced way is that for a man to become a sage, he must first master the Torah which entails mastering both "masculine" and "feminine" ways of thinking. Only then can he become a link in the tradition and a shaper of this tradition. This inherent perfect balance in Judaism demonstrates how its source is none other than He who created male and female.

---

1 Ibid., 944.

Ishah: The Woman's First Name

> Then God, the Lord, built the side that He had taken from
> Adam into a woman, and He brought her to Adam. And
> Adam said, "This time it is bone of my bone, flesh of my
> flesh. This shall be called Woman (*Ishah*), for from Man
> (*Ish*) was she taken."[1]

Both Man and animals were created from the ground, the
adamah. This is why Man is called "Adam." However, only Man
was imbued with fire, *eish*. Fire is a peculiar substance. Whereas
other substances aim to preserve their form, a spark of fire grav-
itates to its source. Fire is the only matter that is always striving
upwards. Fire is also the only substance that can give of itself
and not be diminished. Fire is what drives a person to strive upwards to his/her source, God. It is that part of a person that does
not diminish when a person gives.[2]

When used properly, fire is a positive force. It allows Man to
cook food, it keeps him warm, and it can be used to make sacrifices to God. When not used properly, fire can destroy everything in its path. Likewise, it is this fire which allows a person to
worship God. When not directed to a holy purpose, the fire
drives Man to destruction. One only need to open a history
book or the newspaper for examples of how this fire can be mis-
used.

The words for man, *ish*, and woman, *ishah*, have fire, *eish*, as
their roots. *Eish* is spelled *alef-shin*. *Ish* has the additional letter
yud, and *ishah* has the additional letter *hei*. *Yud-hei* spells God's

---

1 Genesis 2:22–23.
2 Rivkah Slonim, *Total Immersion: A Mikvah Anthology* (Northvale, NJ: Jason
   Aronson, Inc., 1993), xxxiv–xxxv.

name. When a man and woman come together and use their fire properly, they attain holiness. When they misuse their fire, they take out God, the *yud-hei*. All they are left with is a consuming flame that destroys them both.[1]

When the woman was brought to the man, he recognized her as his equal, a complementary partner in life with whom holiness was to be achieved. Therefore, he called her *Ishah*.

The Akeidat Yitzchak, one of the leading rabbis of fifteenth century Spain, makes the following observation on the woman being called *Ishah*:

> The two names "woman" (*ishah*) and "Eve" indicate two purposes. The first teaches that woman was taken from man, stressing that like him you may understand and advance in the intellectual and moral field just as did the matriarchs and many righteous women and prophetesses and as the literal meaning of Proverbs 31 about "the woman of worth" (*eishet chayil*) indicates. The second alludes to the power of childbearing and rearing children, as is indicated by the name Eve — the mother of all living. A woman deprived of the power of childbearing will be deprived of the secondary purpose and be left with the ability to do evil or good like the man who is barren.[2]

In other words, the name *Ishah* refers not only to a woman's joint purpose with her husband, but also to her identity as an individual with personal goals.[3]

---

1 *Sotah* 17b.
2 Nehamah Leibowitz, *New Studies in Bereishit* (Jerusalem: Hemed Press, 1973), 334.
3 Ibid., 335.

Lilith

Considerable attention has been given to Lilith as a role model for the modern woman. In a book titled *The Alphabet of Ben Sira*, Lilith is described as the first woman. She refused to accept the dominion of Adam and flew in a rage out of the Garden of Eden, rebelling against God and becoming a demon who terrorizes Mankind.

Feminists' Interpretations

Feminists view Lilith as a woman who assumed her equality and refused to bow to Adam's attempts to make her subservient. Instead, she chose to fly away from Adam and the Garden of Eden. She chose independence and freedom outside of the Garden of Eden over tyranny and security within it. She did not appeal to God but relied on her own strength. She is powerful, assertive, courageous, passionate. She is a fighter.

While Ben Sira also describes her as a murderer, this part is discounted as false allegations designed by Rabbis to squelch this powerful icon[1] who is so threatening to the patriarchy. In this way, the Rabbis could use this negative image of Lilith as a warning of what will happen to women contemplating their own equality. Lilith also provides feminists a certain comfort that comes from knowing that you are part of a long tradition. With the image of Lilith in the forefront, fighting for equality is transformed from a radical innovation to a continuation of the most ancient struggle.

---

1 A. Cantor, *The Lilith Question*, in *On Being a Jewish Feminist*, Susannah Heschel, ed. (New York: Schocken Books, 1983), 46.

A Critical Look

Although Ben Sira was a Jew from ancient times, many considered him a heretic, and the Talmud says that we should not read his works.[1] It is clear that the story of Lilith does not derive from traditional Jewish sources. Therefore, to say that the Rabbis' portrayal of Lilith is representative of the Rabbinic attitude towards women is absurd.

The "threat" of women's "equality" is more real today than ever in history, so one would expect Rabbis to issue dire warnings to Jewish women contemplating "equality" lest they become like Lilith. One would expect women and men to have at least heard of Lilith and be familiar with her story. Otherwise, she wouldn't be a very effective Rabbinic threat to women who want to be "liberated." However, it has been my personal observation that most women and men who grew up in an Orthodox Jewish environment have never heard of her.

Lilith in the Torah

Masculinity and femininity can be expressed in holy ways and in destructive ways. The destructive expression of masculinity is referred to in the Torah as Samael. We know him well. He is the ultimate megalomaniac dictator who demands complete subservience. His vicious brutality knows no bounds. We have seen him in many world leaders. Tragically, many women and children have seen him in their homes.

The destructive expression of femininity is called Lilith. She represents uncontrollable, devastating lust. We know her well, too. We see her effects in the broken hearts of husbands

---

1 *Sanhedrin* 100b.

and wives who have been betrayed by their spouses. We see her effects in the emaciated bodies and minds of women who try to satisfy society's ideal form for them.

Samael and Lilith are a pair, and they are always together. We see them at work in the drug trade and in the trade in women, where one person's lust is used to finance another's violent quest for power. Ultimately, we see them within ourselves when we are outraged that things did not go our way or when we have impure thoughts.

Women who want role models of strong women who stood up to men to fight for what they believed was right need to look no further than the Torah. Sarah and Rebekah stood up to their husbands, Tamar stood up to Yehudah, Miriam stood up to her father, she and her mother, Yocheved, also defied the Pharaoh, Esther stood up against Haman, Judith stood up to the general who was slaughtering the Jewish people, and the list goes on. Tamar Frankiel's book, *The Voice of Sarah: Feminine Spirituality and Traditional Judaism*, has fascinating in-depth explorations of numerous Jewish heroines.

What Happened in the Garden of Eden

In order to understand the Torah, one must realize that it is neither a history book nor a science book. Its sole purpose is to explain how each person must lead his or her life. The stories which are included in the Torah are therefore not just interesting historical vignettes, but are meant to convey lessons about our current status and how we can elevate ourselves to holiness. Here we will examine the third chapter of Genesis which describes what happened in the Garden of Eden after Adam and

Eve married. This is a key chapter to understand because it is here that we learn about how the world is today and why. Only then can we appreciate how the Torah helps us overcome the current state of reality and recreate at least in some way the life Man had in the Garden of Eden.

> And God, the Lord, commanded the man [Adam], saying, "Of every tree of the garden you may freely eat; but of the Tree of Knowledge of Good and Evil, you must not eat thereof; for on the day you eat of it, you shall surely die."...
>
> They were both naked, the man and his wife, and they were not ashamed.
>
> Now the serpent was cunning beyond any beast of the field that God, the Lord, had made. He said to the woman, "Did perhaps, God say: 'You shall not eat of any tree of the garden'?"[1]

Who or what was this serpent? In order to answer this question, we must step back and look at the very purpose of Creation. We know nothing about God Himself — He is completely beyond human comprehension. The only thing we can even begin to understand is His relationship to His Creation. Even this we are only able to know because God Himself told us.

God is a perfect unity in every way. He is independent of everything and He does not need anything. He created the world not because He was lacking, but because He wanted to give. Creation was thus an act of pure love. God wanted to give only the ultimate good. The ultimate good is God Himself. God is the very definition of good. Therefore, the greatest good that God could give is Himself. In other words, the greatest good that a

---

1 Genesis 2:16–17, 25, 3:1.

person can get is to cling to God.

How is this possible? It is not possible in the physical sense, but it is in the spiritual sense. In the spiritual world, two things are considered close to each other when they resemble each other. An example of this in the physical world is in the field of mathematics. In the physical world, sound, ocean waves, and triangles may not seem to have anything in common. However, the equations that describe the angles of a triangle, the motion of the sound waves, and the motion of ocean waves are all variations of a sine function. The form of the function is the same for all three apparently different things. Therefore, on a mathematical level, one can view all these things as similar. Likewise, in the spiritual world, when two things resemble each other, they are said to be similar. Therefore, the way to be close to God is to emulate Him.

If God is always giving to Man, and Man is receiving, then Man becomes the exact opposite of God, since a giver and receiver are opposites. Therefore, God had to give Man a means of giving to Him. Although everything is in God's control, He gave Man control over his own fear of God. That is, He gave him free will. When a person uses his free will to act in a way that shows his awe of God, he is using his God-given abilities to give back to God. He is becoming a giver and emulating God to the fullest degree possible.

It is not enough for Man to have free will, he also has to have the opportunity to use it. For this reason, God had to "hide" Himself so that His presence would not be readily apparent. If a person always felt that God was right there, he would be too scared to do anything wrong. His ability to use his free will would be curtailed. Also, free will is of little use when there are no choices to make. Therefore, God created an alternative choice, that is, evil, in order to allow Man to exercise his free will.

When Adam and Eve were created, they did not have an internal evil inclination. It was an external force they had to overcome. This was personified by the snake. Before the sin, the snake was a very different creature. He had hands and feet and walked upright. He was meant to be Adam's servant. In other words, the evil inclination would be something Adam and Eve had mastered and which could help them to serve God. But first, the snake had to fulfill his role of presenting a choice to Adam and Eve as an alternative to listening to God. Adam and Eve were meant to turn away from the wrong choice, use their free will to follow God's commandment, and fulfill the purpose of Creation. The challenge would have been met once and for all, and they could look forward to living eternally in Paradise.

In Genesis 2:25, Adam and Eve are described as "naked," *arum*. Now the Torah describes the serpent using the exact same word, *arum*, yet here it means "cunning" or "subtle." As Rabbi Hertz explains, this is because "[s]eeming simplicity is often the most dangerous weapon of cunning."[1] Indeed, the snake starts his seduction with a seemingly innocuous question about the scope of God's prohibition.

> The woman said to the serpent, "We may eat of the fruit of the trees of the garden. Of the tree which is in the center of the garden God has said: 'You shall neither eat of it nor touch it, lest you die.'"[2]

---

1 *Hertz Chumash*, commentary to Genesis 3:1 (Soncino Press, 1936).
2 Genesis 3:2–3.

Let us compare what Eve relates to what God actually said. As Nehamah Leibowitz points out, Eve minimized what was permitted, magnified what was forbidden, and minimized the consequences of transgression.[1] God's statement, "Of every tree in the garden you may freely eat," becomes "We may eat of the fruit of the trees of the garden." God's generosity and encouragement to partake of His goodness is absent from Eve's statement.

Likewise, she greatly magnified what was prohibited. The tree which stood in a corner of the garden suddenly seems to be in the "center" of the garden for Eve. Its importance is thereby greatly enlarged. Then, she adds to the prohibition by saying that even touching the tree is forbidden, which God never said. One reason given for her addition is that it was Adam who told it to her.[2] The commandment was given to Adam before Eve was created, and Adam related it to her. However, he arrogantly assumed that just telling her what God actually said would not be enough for her, so he added the prohibition of touching the tree. He did not mention that this was his own addition, but presented it as part of God's commandment.

The Sages instruct us to "build a fence around the Torah,"[3] meaning that we must refrain from doing things which might lead to violating a commandment. In addition, the Torah states that one may not add nor subtract from the commandments.[4] The "fences" that are built must be presented as "fences" to guard the commandments, and not as commandments themselves. Therefore, Adam's prohibition against touching the tree <u>was in line with how one should</u> approach commandments. His

---

1 Leibowitz, *New Studies in Bereishit*, 30.

2 M. Weissman, ed., *The Midrash Says: The Book of Beraishis* (New York: Benei Yaakov Publications, 1980), 45.

3 *Avot* 1:1.

4 Deuteronomy 13:1.

error was omitting the fact that it was his idea, not God's. Instead, he presented his addition as being of equal stature to God's commandment. This was a result of his arrogance both toward Eve and toward God. When the Torah was given to the Jewish people, it was taught directly to the women in order not to replicate Adam's mistake.

Eve proceeds to minimize the outcome of eating from the tree. Whereas God said, "For on the day you eat of it, you shall surely die," Eve said, "You shall neither eat of it nor touch it, lest you die." As Nehamah Leibowitz points out, "What originally constituted in the Almighty's wording, a moral connection between the sin and the punishment is transformed by the woman into a mere mechanical link of cause and effect."[1] Furthermore, the forceful "you will surely die" is whittled down to "lest you die."

The snake then pushed Eve against the tree and said, "Just as you did not die from touching it, so you will no die from eating it!"[2] At this point, Eve should have gone to Adam for clarification and not assumed that she could now ignore everything he told her.

> The serpent said to the woman, "You will not surely die; for God knows that on the day you eat of it your eyes will be opened and you will be like God, knowing good and evil."[3]

Here, the Torah describes the way a tempter works. First, he enlarges the scope of the prohibition until it seems impossible

---

1 Leibowitz, *New Studies in Bereishit,* 31.
2 Midrash on Genesis 3:3.
3 Genesis 3:4–5.

to observe it — the snake asked Eve if all the trees were forbidden. Then, he flat out denies the consequences of transgression: "You will not surely die." The snake's next step is far more insidious — he implies that the commandment is not for her own benefit, but for God's! As Rabbi Hirsch says, "[The snake said that] God did not prohibit this tree out of any concern for your lives, but because He is aware that by eating from it you will attain extra wisdom and become omniscient like Him. Then you will be independent of Him."[1]

The snake's statement is ludicrous. The only reason the world was created was for Man's benefit, and God wants him to enjoy it to the maximum. God is then presented as jealously guarding His unique status from an encroaching Man. This is reminiscent of the gods of Greek and Roman mythology, and anathema to Jewish thought.

Finally, the snake promises Eve that she will know good and evil. This was actually quite a sophisticated argument — eating from the Tree of Knowledge would allow Eve to fulfill her role by being better able to emulate God. Eve should have been able to see the fallacy of this reasoning — she would not be able to emulate God if she was disobeying Him.[2] Furthermore, Adam and Eve already possessed the ability to discern what was morally right and wrong because they were formed in God's image.

And the woman perceived that the tree was good for eating and that it was a delight to the eyes, and that the tree was desirable as a means to wisdom, and she took of its fruit and ate; and she gave also to her husband with her and he ate.[3]

---

1 Rabbi Hirsch, commentary on Genesis 3:4–5.
2 Kaplan, *Inner Space*, 88.
3 Genesis 3:6.

It is ironic that the word that is translated as "as a means to wisdom" is *maskil*. The way it is conjugated, it really means "to make wise." The root of the word is *haskalah*, enlightenment, which is also what the Jewish "Enlightenment" of the nineteenth century was called.

For centuries, the Jews of eastern and western Europe lived in ghettos. They were excluded from society in all areas – social, economic, political. They were at the mercy of the rulers, and sometimes at the mercy of angry mobs who wanted to exact revenge from them for killing their god. Their choices for professions were very limited. Usually they were delegated to do the dirty work that gentiles thought was beneath them, like money lending. The rulers subjected them to all sorts of injustices to degrade and humiliate them. Within the ghettos, however, they had self-rule. They had their own rabbinic courts who would judge according to Jewish law and whose decisions were binding.

This all changed with the Enlightenment. The Enlightenment was a movement active in Europe from the late 1700s to the late 1800s. It transformed Europe from a composite of medieval kingdoms to a conglomeration of modern countries. The god of the Enlightenment was Reason. No longer would man be a slave to superstitions, and no longer would he blindly accept some absolute authority. A man of Reason had the right to question everything, to determine his own course in life, and only be ruled by those whom he chose. The ideas of the universal rights of man, self-government, and citizenship and the resulting French Revolution and American Revolution are products of the Enlightenment.

The Enlightenment was great for Europe. It was disastrous for the Jews. Under the new order, the Jew was able to come out of the ghetto and become a fully integrated member of society, at least theoretically, without having to convert. The Jews could attend the universities and get the best education in the arts and sciences. All the professions were suddenly open to them. There was just one catch: they had to forsake the Torah.

The Haskalah was the Jewish version of the Enlightenment. Its members, called *maskilim*, took the principles of Reason and attempted to judge the Torah by its standard. Instead of revering the Torah as the word of an omniscient God as revealed to finite Man, the *maskilim* revered the infinite Man who would now judge the Torah and decide what he liked and what he wanted to discard as mere superstitions. In *Sulamith*, a newspaper of the Haskalah, the author wrote, "The task of religious enlightenment is to illuminate and elucidate the concept of man regarding religious truths, the existence of the Creator, providence, immortality, etc., and to clarify man's religious creed and free it from the additions and abuses of harmful fanaticisms and foolish prejudices.... Enlightenment banishes the low, slavish fear of the world's Ruler from our hearts."[1]

The *maskilim*'s view of Judaism varied from it being complete superstition to an already enlightened religion which just needed a little adjustment. But they all agreed that the Haskalah and the promise of assimilation of Jews into general society took precedence. The result of the modernization was that the majority of Jews left Torah-observant Judaism, many to be lost forever.

Eve saw that the "tree was good for eating and that it was a delight to the eyes, and that the tree was desirable as a means to

---

1   Anonymous, *Sulamith* 2 (Leipzig, 1808), 221–22. Translated by M. Gelber, as cited in P. Mendes-Flohr and J. Reinharz, ed., *The Jew in the Modern World: A Documentary History* (New York: Oxford University Press, 1980), 76.

wisdom (*l'haskil*)." Indeed it was. The decision lay before her: would she throw off the yoke of God's command and eat this fruit? Like the *maskilim*, that is exactly what she did.

It wasn't until the late 1800s that a man named Rabbi Samson Raphael Hirsch championed the idea that one could be a member of society and committed to living a Torah life. Torah Judaism, however, could never be compromised. If the choice was between working on the Sabbath or losing a job, you observe the Sabbath. Instead of eating nonkosher foods to fit into society, you keep kosher.

God would have given Adam and Eve the fruit anyway on that Sabbath.[1] He waited in order to give them an opportunity to show their obedience to Him and proclaim His sovereignty. Then, they would attain the wisdom they were looking for. If they had placed God's commandment above their own desires, they would have achieved the goal for which the world was created.

After having eaten the fruit herself, Eve also gave some to her husband who was "*imah*," "with her," which can also be translated as "at one with her."[2] That is, he was positively involved in the sin and not helplessly overwhelmed by Eve.

> Then the eyes of both of them were opened and they realized that they were naked; and they sewed together fig leaves and made themselves aprons.[3]

The serpent was right about one thing — their eyes would be opened when they would eat of the fruit. But instead of attaining

---

1 ArtScroll Tanach Series, *Bereishis,* vol. 1 (New York: Mesorah Publications, Ltd., 1978), 18.

2 *Radak* and *Ibn Ezra* commentaries on Genesis 3:6.

3 Genesis 3:7.

wisdom like he promised, they attained shame. When Adam and Eve looked at each other before the sin, they saw each other's soul. The body was completely dedicated to leading a holy life and there was nothing to be ashamed of. After the sin, the body became divorced from the soul. When Adam and Eve looked at each other, they only saw each other's body because it had eclipsed the soul. In other words, they couldn't help but objectify each other. They perceived each other as well as themselves as an object, a body, instead of a human being in God's image. This was especially true with regard to their sexual organs. This was very embarrassing for them, and so they quickly made clothes to cover themselves.

This is the reality till this day. Even in places where there is no utilitarian need for clothing, such as in hot climates, people always wear a minimum of clothing which covers their sexual organs. The emphasis in Judaism on modesty in clothing and behavior for men and women is meant to constructively deal with this reality so that when a man and woman look at each other, they can see each other's soul.

> They heard the sound of Hashem God manifesting Itself in the garden toward evening; and the man and his wife hid from Hashem God among the trees of the garden. Hashem God called out to the man and said to him, "Where are you?"[1]

No lightning bolt came down as soon as Eve or Adam sinned. They were not immediately killed or punished in any way. In fact, quite a lot happened between the sin and the expulsion. First, they were given time to make clothes for themselves

1 Ibid., 8–9.

and dress themselves. From here we learn a lesson in etiquette: one should not look upon a man in his disgrace.[1] Then, they heard "the sound of Hashem God manifesting Itself in the garden" and they hid behind a tree. Shame made them cowards.

God then called out to Adam, "Where are you?" Was God unaware of Adam's whereabouts? Of course He knew where he was. However, what God really wanted was not to punish Adam and Eve but for them to repent. He therefore gave them numerous opportunities to admit their wrong and ask forgiveness. First He waited till they clothed themselves, then He let them know of His arrival, and now He asks Adam, "Where are you?" God was not asking Adam of his physical location, but of his spiritual location, that is, "Consider well how you have fallen from the heights; where is your exalted status?"[2] When the word for "Where are you," "*ayekah*," is vowelized differently, it can read "*eichah*," which is like a mourning sigh. Here, God was expressing His sadness over what Adam had done, as well as giving him an opportunity to admit his sin and repent.

> He said, "I heard the sound of You in the garden, and I was afraid because I am naked, so I hid."
> And He said, "Who told you that you are naked? Have you eaten of the tree from which I commanded you not to eat?' "[3]

Instead of taking advantage of the opportunity, Adam gives a lame answer. God gives him another try to confess, this time practically putting the words into his mouth: "Have you eaten of the tree from which I commanded you not to eat?" Here the tree

---

1 Weissman, *The Midrash Says*, 50.
2 *Aderet Eliyahu* commentary on Genesis 3:9.
3 Genesis 3:10–11.

is referred to by its most relevant title as "the tree from which I commanded you not to eat." It does not matter that it was the tree of knowledge, or whether it was in the midst of the garden. It was the tree whose fruit God prohibited and He emphasizes that in His question.

> The man said, "The woman whom You gave to be with me – she gave me of the tree, and I ate."[1]

Adam really blew it here. Instead of admitting that he was wrong, he blamed everyone else. First, he blamed Eve. Then he blamed God because it was He who gave her to him. This showed a complete lack of gratitude to God for giving him such a treasure. Lack of gratitude is considered a very serious sin. By not expressing thankfulness, one hurts the person's feelings and makes him feel unappreciated and unimportant. But the more corrupting aspect of this sin is what it does to oneself. If one is not careful about training himself to always acknowledge what others do for him, he comes to take all their efforts for granted. Their giving is seen as simply the "natural order of things" for which one need not be any more grateful than for the force of gravity for keeping one from floating into space. One also starts to think that everything he has accomplished was exclusively due to his own efforts. This makes him believe that he is self-sufficient, completely independent of all others and ultimately of God. This attitude is idolatry where the idol is oneself.

A key ingredient in the creation of Man is speech. Speech is the means by which Man expresses his intellect to the world. The Torah describes how God created the world through ten "sayings." While this is an anthropomorphism, this does teach us a valuable lesson. Just like God used speech to create the

1   Ibid., 12.

world, so too can Man use his speech to parallel God's act of creation. Man can also use his speech to effect a parallel act of destruction.

By implicating Eve in the iniquity, Adam committed another lethal error – the sin of *lashon hara*, evil speech. *Lashon hara* is something which 1) is true, 2) one knows with absolute certainty,[1] 3) might be interpreted in a negative manner about the subject,[2] 4) not absolutely necessary for the listener to know.[3] There is a story in the Talmud[4] about Rabbi Alexandri, who called out in the street, "Who wants life? Who wants life?" Soon, a large crowd gathered around him, expecting him to offer some wonderful drug. Instead, he quoted Psalms (31:13–14), "Who is the man who desires life and loves days that he may see the good? Guard your tongue from evil and your lips from speaking deceit." He was teaching that observing the laws of *lashon hara* is a matter of life and death.

One might argue that it's okay to say *lashon hara* to God because He already knows everything and will not think any lower

---

1 If saying something that is true and that one is absolutely sure of is such a serious transgression, how much more so when one spreads lies or things which are based on hearsay.

2 One must be very careful even about saying positive things about people because it might lead to trouble (e.g., "Mrs. Cohen is so generous with her time." "Really? Yesterday I asked her for a favor and she told me she was too busy").

3 There are times when one is obligated to say negative things about another. For example, if someone is considering a business partnership with a person you are acquainted with, he may legitimately ask you for your assessment of his character. If there are aspects of his character that are negative which you have good reason to believe will affect the partnership, you are obligated to mention them. Given the gravity and complexity of observing these laws correctly, one should study the laws carefully. A very helpful and highly readable book is *Guard Your Tongue* by Rabbi Zelig Pliskin (New York: Benei Yaakov Publication, 1975).

4 *Avodah Zarah* 19b.

of the subject of *lashon hara*. However, this reasoning is not correct. The reason we must observe commandments is not for the sake of others, but for our own sake. For example, an individual is forbidden to steal because stealing is bad for that individual, not because stealing disrupts the smooth functioning of a society, and not even because it hurts people. Therefore, if stealing had no effect on anyone else, it would still be forbidden. The hurt that one causes to others through stealing compounds the sin further. *Lashon hara* is forbidden regardless of what effect it has on the subject or the listener. Therefore, one must be very careful about what one says about others, even to God.

A situation in which one is obligated to say something negative about another is when one is being questioned in a court. One might argue that Adam had a right to implicate Eve because God was questioning him as if he was in a court of law. However, God only asked him who told him he was naked and if he ate from the tree. Mentioning Eve was completely unnecessary.

The two things which distinguish a human as being in the image of God are free will and the power of speech. With one statement, Adam abused his power of speech by saying *lashon hara*, and he denied that he had free will by blaming Eve and God. His claim was that he did not possess the ability to control his actions, therefore he should not be held responsible for them. He thus denied that he was made in God's image and lowered himself below all the animals.

Men continue to commit these sins today when they blame Eve, and by extension all women, for the evil that exists in the world. They even use the Torah as "proof" to justify their vilification of women. However, the Torah makes it clear that God did not accept Adam's excuse and held him accountable. By relying on the excuse, Adam precluded his own repentance. Likewise, when men repeat Adam's words today, they are perpetuating evil.

Adam's chutzpah did not end there. The Sages note that his last statement, "and I ate," is actually conjugated in the future tense, meaning "I ate, and I would eat again in the future!"[1] There was nothing more that God could do at this point to help Adam repent.

> And Hashem God said to the woman, "What is this that you have done!"
>
> The woman said, "The serpent deceived me, and I ate."[2]

God then turns His attention to Eve. Whereas He asks Adam three questions to encourage him to repent, He directs only one statement towards Eve to give her one chance to repent. One reason for this may be that Eve not only sinned herself, but influenced Adam to sin as well. Influencing someone else to do something is even more powerful than doing something oneself, and this works both ways. When one encourages someone to do a good deed, then one gets even more credit than the person doing the good deed. Likewise, encouraging someone to sin is an even greater offense than committing the sin oneself. Eve was created to be an *ezer k'negdo*, to influence Adam for the good, and she perverted her role.

Eve had the opportunity to learn from Adam's mistake, and she could have repented. However, she repeated his sins by denying her own free will, speaking *lashon hara* about the snake,

---

1 Rabbi Nosson Scherman and Rabbi Meir Zlotowitz, ed., *The Chumash* (New York: Mesorah Publications, 1996), 17.

2 Genesis 3:13.

and then boldly declaring that she too was ready to eat of the fruit in the future.

> And Hashem God said to the serpent, "Because you have done this, accursed are you beyond all the cattle and beyond all beasts of the field; upon your belly shall you go, and dust shall you eat all the days of your life. I will put enmity between you and the woman, and between your offspring and her offspring. He will pound your head, and you will bite his heel."[1]

If the snake was only doing his job, then why was he punished? In the *Zohar* there is a parable of a king who wanted to test his son's loyalty.[2] First the king told his son not to go near any loose women. He then hired a woman to entice him. Once the prince saw through the disguise he became immune to her charm. Now say the woman were to tell him that he should be with her because that is what his father really wants. This ceases to be a test of loyalty, and instead becomes a mind game which is not what the king wanted. Instead of presenting Eve with the choice between good and evil, the snake presented evil as good and as the only way to fulfill God's plan. He went beyond his role and thus sinned.

God did not give the serpent a chance to defend himself because he influenced Eve and Adam to usurp God's rule over them, which is idolatry. When one commits a sin for which one is liable for the death penalty, as Adam and Eve did, he is given a chance to defend himself in court. However, if the sin in question is leading others to idolatry, then he is not given the chance

---

1 Ibid., 14–15.
2 *Zohar* 2:163a, as quoted in Kaplan, *Inner Space*, 84, 88.

to defend himself.[1] God immediately curses the snake beyond all the other animals. His arms and legs are cut off. The next statement, "dust shall you eat," does not seem like much of a curse.[2] Dust is found everywhere and the snake should never have any trouble finding food. However, the flip side of this is that the snake would never have to pray to God for food either. God wanted nothing to do with the snake and made it as self-sufficient as possible.

The snake tried to get Eve to sin by appealing to her head, her intellect. When she sinned, and again when she influenced Adam to sin, she and Adam were lowered below their heels. That is, their subsequent spiritual statures were on a much lower level than even the "heel" of their previous selves. Therefore, God reverses the situation by decreeing that from then on the snake would only strike at Man's heel, while Man would strike at the snake's head. This puts the snake at a permanent disadvantage and sentences him to always be crushed by Man.

> To the woman He said, "I will greatly increase your suffering and your childbearing; in pain shall you bear children. Yet your craving shall be for your husband, and he shall rule over you."[3]

When a person wants to strengthen a muscle, she exercises it. An effective exercise is one that will challenge the muscle. It will feel unpleasant and be difficult to do, but in the end it will

---

1 Weissman, *The Midrash Says,* 53.
2 This may seem to contradict the fact that snakes do not eat dust but live animals. However, remember that the Torah is not meant to be a science text, but a moral guide. What is meant is that all the food that the snake eats will taste like dust. See Weissman, *The Midrash Says,* 55.
3 Genesis 3:16.

make the muscle stronger. When Adam and Eve sinned, they weakened their spiritual muscles. In order to help them regain their strength, God had to give them "exercises" — obstacles and challenges to help them grow to their spiritual potential. Since Adam and Eve sinned in somewhat different ways, they had to be given distinct obstacles.

Eve thought that she could be independent of God. Therefore, God altered her body so that it would constantly remind her of just how little control she had.[1] Before the sin, Eve would give birth immediately and painlessly to an adult child without nine months of pregnancy. This is how Cain and Abel were born. She would now menstruate every month, an uncomfortable experience. Before giving birth, she would have a nine-month pregnancy which could range from being uncomfortable to being debilitating. Then, she would have intense pain in giving birth to the child. Sometimes she would suffer a miscarriage. Raising the child would be physically and emotionally draining. After everything she went through, she still had no control over how her child would develop.

All these changes serve to remind the woman of her dependence on God. Raising children are reminders to her of just how dependent she is on God. She prays to God that He make her feel well, that He give her an easy pregnancy, that He help her get through labor, that the child be healthy, that He give her the strength to take care of the child, that the child grow up to be a righteous person, and so on. All these changes become springboards to petitions and conversations with God, and they help her make Him an intimate and constant companion.

The Torah provides a way for a woman to overcome these difficulties, or at least to lessen them. When a woman is very

1   Weissman, *The Midrash Says,* 56.

careful about fulfilling the three commandments especially incumbent on women – taking challah, lighting Shabbat candles, and following the laws of *niddah* – her labor pains diminish. Very righteous women, like the women in Egypt and in the wilderness, did not experience labor pains.[1] But a woman does not have to be on that level of righteousness to experience relief. She only has to believe in God, put her whole faith in Him, and realize that everything that happens is according to His will, and therefore ultimately good. This alone can comfort her even in the most trying times and give her the strength to get through her travails.

This attitude also helps when raising children. Many mothers feel that they are personally responsible for everything concerning their child. This includes the child's behavior and the kind of person he or she becomes. My child behaved badly in school? It must be my fault. My child did not get into the best university? I must have done something wrong. Even when mothers can intellectually distinguish between things they can and cannot control, emotionally the two are perceived in the same way. This makes the already difficult job of mothering impossible. By constantly reminding herself that it is God, not she, who is in charge, a woman can stop feeling responsible for things beyond her control and instead concentrate on what she can control.

One way the sages interpreted "Yet your craving shall be for your husband" is that in spite of the pain and difficulty of having children, the woman will still want to have relations and be a mother. In fact, being a mother is a stronger instinct in women than survival. Even though a woman will want to be with her husband, she will have difficulty expressing her needs. Jewish

1 Ibid.

law understands this and commands the husband to be very attentive to his wife so that he would meet her needs without her having to verbalize them.

"[H]e shall rule over you" — one might argue that this is the root of the patriarchy which has been oppressing women since the dawn of civilization. However, it is interesting to note what the Torah does not say as much as what it does. Here, God is not addressing Adam, telling him that he now can or should rule over his wife. Nor does God tell Eve that she must submit to his rule. He also does not say that Adam can abuse or oppress Eve. Rather, He is stating how life would be, not how it should be. Indeed, this has been a fact of life which has only very recently been contested.

It makes sense that a husband would rule his wife after the sin. He is physically stronger, and his wife depends on him financially because all her time is spent on child-rearing and housekeeping. This is true even today when modern appliances and disposable diapers revolutionized housework and caring for a baby. Women are still at an economic disadvantage to men even when they work outside the home because they take time off to take care of their babies and take less stressful (and lower paying) jobs so they can continue to take care of their children. Once the evil inclination become a part of man, he could easily use his advantage to dominate and exploit his wife. However, this was never permitted by God.

Eve used her influence over her husband inappropriately and caused him to sin. Now, she would be ruled by him.[1] This is something which the Torah law corrects. A man is commanded to treat his wife with love and respect. He is not allowed to say a cross word to her, let alone abuse her. He also has to provide her

1   *Ramban* commentary to Genesis 3:16.

with all her daily needs, including things like makeup and jewelry. The Torah also guides the wife to be a true *ezer k'negdo*, a positive influence on her husband.

> To Adam He said, "Because you listened to the voice of your wife and ate of the tree about which I commanded you saying, 'You shall not eat of it,' accursed is the ground because of you; through suffering shall you eat of it all the days of your life. Thorns and thistles shall it sprout for you, and you shall eat the herb of the field. By the sweat of your brow shall you eat bread until you return to the ground, from which you were taken: For you are dust, and to dust shall you return."[1]

Adam was punished for listening to his wife's voice without examining her words.[2] The phrase "listen to the voice" occurs in a couple of other places in the Torah. We looked at one example where God told Abraham to listen to Sarah's voice, even when her words did not make sense to him. Another example is when Rebekah, our second foremother, instructed Jacob to pretend he was Esau and get his father's blessing that was reserved for the firstborn. When Jacob objected that his father might discover his true identity, Rebekah told him to "listen to her voice."[3] What she said may not have made sense, but it was the right thing to do. In this way, our foremothers demonstrated how all future Jewish women can use their voices to influence the world for the good.

The changes to the world which made Adam's labor very difficult parallel the changes in Eve's labor. Earning a livelihood

1 Genesis 3:17–19.
2 *Or HaChaim* commentary to Genesis 3:17.
3 Genesis 27:13.

would from then on be very arduous. It would also be largely out of Adam's control. Adam would have to constantly turn to God and pray that he be able to feed his family and meet all their needs. He would also need to put in a lot of hours and be away from his wife a lot. He listened to Eve because he was too attached to her. Now he would be forced to separate from her for long periods of time.

It is interesting to note that although both Adam and Eve were punished with death, the Torah lists this as a punishment for Adam. "For you are dust, and to dust shall you return" – this is every man's fear – that he is nothing and that he will never amount to anything.[1] In order to combat this fear, men keep trying to prove that they are men, that they are someone. Some men do this by conquering countries and naming cities after themselves. Others acquire property and name buildings and streets after themselves. Others acquire wealth. Others conquer women. In more primitive cultures, boys have to go through some ordeal in order to become men in the eyes of the tribe. In American culture, sports is the medium through which many boys learn about manhood and prove that they are men. The logic is that if you have (something) or do (something), then you are (someone).

The Torah shows men how they can be someone important by using the above logic in a positive way. What a man needs to acquire in order to be a man are mitzvot and Torah learning. As it says in the Torah, "Ben Zoma says: Who is wise? He who learns from every person.... Who is strong? He who is able to conquer his [evil] inclination. As it says: 'Better is the patient person than the strong person, and better is the person who can rule over his temper than the person who can capture a city.'

1 Manis Friedman, *Beyond the Male Ego* (cassette tape).

Who is rich? He who is happy with his lot.... Who is honored? He who honors mankind...."[1] In order to become a real man, a man also needs a wife.[2] Not scores of women whom he conquered, but a single woman with whom he will unite and become whole. In this way the Torah takes everything men try to get to prove their importance and channels it in a positive way.

Women do not have the same fear that there will not be anything left of them after they are gone. A person binds herself to what she gave the most of herself to and to that for which she suffered. The only way in which a person can achieve immortality now is through her children. When a parent throws herself into raising her child, then she continues to live through her child even after her death. All her efforts in taking care of the child and teaching him continue to bear fruit even after she is gone. By making raising children very difficult and painful from pregnancy onward, God precluded death from being the threat to a woman's feelings of self-worth. A woman who raises her children is confident that her efforts, her very self, will live on after she is gone. It is obvious to her that what she accomplished is important and will endure.

Men can certainly exert great effort in raising their children and reap the benefits for doing so. However, they physically cannot do this to the extent that a woman can. Furthermore, their having to earn a livelihood will limit how much they can be with their children. For men, there are no guarantees that what they do will outlive them. The Torah corrects this by commanding men to have children and by giving fathers the responsibility of teaching Torah to their children. While biology limits what a man can do to bring a child into this world, his ability to bring

---

1   *Avot* 4:1.

2   *Yevamot* 63a.

his children to the world to come is unlimited. The Torah commands men to use this ability. In this way, men are shown how to truly achieve immortality so that they, too, can face death in peace.

Most people believe that they are really good at heart. Yet there is still a lot of evil in the world. Even people with the best of intentions are capable of an enormous amount of evil, often because of their best intentions. The Tree of Knowledge of Good and Evil had fruit where good and evil were so intertwined as to be indistinguishable from each other. When Adam and Eve ate this fruit, they internalized this complete mix of good and evil. Now good could be disguised as evil, and evil could be disguised as good. Illusion became a fact of life. In fact, it is not exactly evil that causes destruction but illusion — the belief that one is actually doing something good. People generally have a hard time devoting themselves to something which they know is wrong, but they can become fanatics about something which they think is right. For example, the Nazis really believed that what they were doing was good. They were ridding the world of its parasites and establishing their own superior race.

God gave us the Torah in order to allow us to go outside of our own (mis)perception of reality and connect us to the true reality. By studying God's will and doing His commandments, we are able to once again distinguish between good and evil and banish illusion. We are able to do this to a limited degree now, but when the Messiah comes we will be able to see reality with complete clarity.

Chapter 3

Modesty

For a woman, Judaism stresses modesty and her role in the family. Many women find this offensive. Images come to mind of a submissive, self-effacing woman whose entire life is confined to her claustrophobically small domestic sphere. Her sexuality is in a straitjacket that the 1960s gleefully tore apart in the rest of the modern world. However, these images have nothing to do with the Jewish picture.

Modesty for men and women is one of the most important qualities valued in Judaism, yet it is often the most misunderstood. Modesty is the translation for two words: *tzeniut* and *anavah*. On the most superficial level, *tzeniut* means not dressing in a suggestive manner. Dressing provocatively has become more than a way to be fashionable or attract the attention of the opposite sex. As society broke away from the repressive "sex is taboo" mentality, exposing and wielding one's sexuality has become a banner proclaiming personal liberation. This has been particularly true for women. To return to standards of dress that are meant to conceal one's sexuality seems like a throwback to Victorian times.

Judaism recognizes that sexual feelings are healthy emotions for both women and men. In the proper context, intimacy is not only considered good but vital for a person's well-being. Judaism pays particular attention to a woman's needs and obligates her husband to fulfill them. Sexual repression is not the goal of modest dress. In Judaism, modesty in dress, which is required of women as well as men, is a means of liberation. Yes, liberation.

The Antithesis of Objectification

Objectification is generally associated with dirty men looking at pornographic pictures. What makes this act so galling is that a complex human being is reduced to a thing. But objectification need not be obvious to be potent. It can exist in many subtle ways, like when a person wears revealing clothing. If she just happens to be wearing what is in fashion, then she confirms the creed of couture that her body is the source of her beauty. In a culture where a woman's beauty is the source of much of her value, she also confirms that her body is the source of her value. If she uses her body as a means of attracting attention, then the first message that is sent is "Look at what a beautiful thing I am." If flaunting her sexuality is self-expression, then the message becomes confined by the limits of her body. On the other hand, wearing nonrevealing clothing allows a person to be fashionable and express herself without first having to chip away at her humanity.

There are many practical advantages to dressing modestly. A person is under no pressure to expose his or her body to the tyranny of public scrutiny. No more jeans that don't let you sit, eat, and breathe all at the same time. No more miniskirts that ride up too high or blouses that go too low when you move slightly. There is no longer any reason to lose sleep over how one will look in a bathing suit or swimming trunks (although the latter is far more forgiving than the former). No more worries about imperfect thighs, not quite washboard stomachs, or less than firm arms. Liberation has begun!

Objectification is not limited to using sex as a way to reduce a person into an object. Any external factor, such as wealth or social standing, will suffice as a weapon. An example is how people treat an "unpopular" person. This person could be cruelly teased and shamelessly physically harassed because the tormentors don't think this person has feelings like everyone else. It's okay to be mean to this person because it's "just" So-and-So. He doesn't count.

Objectification also does not necessarily intend to demean the objectified person. For example, a millionaire could be idolized simply because of his affluence. He may be a nasty person who cheated many, but people may adore him for his fortune. He may receive "honor" due to the objectification. However, this "honor" is false since it stems from the belief that he is something less than human, a money bag.

Tzeniut is the antithesis of objectification. It is the realization that a person's true worth comes from within. It is when one's sense of worth stems not from external factors such as her figure, wealth, or social standing. Rather, it is based entirely on actions and inner qualities. Public recognition for its own sake then becomes irrelevant. Modesty is the understanding that beauty cannot be plastered on. True beauty must stem from one's deeds, speech, and thought, and it radiates from the inside out. This is a beauty which age can only enhance.

By dressing modestly, one cannot use one's body as a way to define oneself to others. Others' perceptions influence self-perception which in turn affects self-definition. In this way, the body becomes very limited in how much of one's self-image it constitutes. Consequently, one must look to one's inner aspects to form a self-image. The concentration on one's own inner beauty leads to an appreciation of others' inner beauty. One ceases to objectify others and sees each person as nothing less than a full human being. This is the beginning of the other meaning of modesty, *anavah*.

Anavah can be understood as the antithesis of pride, *ga'avah*. When one has *ga'avah*, one's self-evaluation is far above one's true self. *Anavah* then means having an accurate assessment of one's self. With *anavah*, one does not consider oneself better than others. Maybe one is especially gifted in particular areas, but that only increases one's responsibility in those areas. A person with *anavah* considers herself overall no better than others. Combined with *tzeniut*, *anavah* results in having a fair evaluation of one's self based on one's actions, speech, and thoughts.

The essence of Jewish thought is the belief in one God who is the embodiment of good and who is intimately concerned with each person's life. *Tzeniut* is a ramification of this belief. Knowing there is Someone who sees everything and who will duly reward and punish gives a person the strength to be independent of others' judgments and to rely solely on God for approval. To be independent of other people for self-definition and to judge oneself only according to how one performs the will of a just and merciful God, that is true liberation.

Tzeniut can have far-reaching implications for a person's self-image. Many people become so engrossed by what they do or by how they relate to others that they forget who they are. Consider the stockbroker who works one hundred hours a week. When asked, "Who are you?" he or she will say, "a stockbroker." When asked, "Yes, but *who* are you?" he or she will have to admit, "I don't know." *Tzeniut* demands that a person maintain an individual relationship with God that goes beyond external factors such as professional and familial status. This helps a person always remember who he or she is: a human being made in God's image.

Tzeniut in the Man's Path

People are generally much more familiar with the path given to men. The man praying with his tefillin (phylacteries) and tallit (prayer shawl) is the image that most often comes to mind when one thinks of a traditional Jew. The *kippah* (skullcap), which is worn only by men, proclaims to the world that he is a Jew. This is no accident since men were given the public role in Judaism. It is their responsibility to go out in the world and proclaim God's sovereignty. In the Jewish nation, they are the ambassadors to the world.

While the Torah sends men into the public sphere, it never lets them forget why they are put there: to sanctify God's name. Positions of public power can easily be used as an opportunity for prestige and wealth. But as our Sages have warned, "He who seeks to make his name great will lose his name.... He who uses the crown of Torah for his own gain will perish."[1]

It often goes unremarked by observers that men are obligated to dress and act with *tzeniut*. Perhaps the biggest reason is

---

1   *Avot* 1:13.

because secular society's standards for men's dress is not very different from those of Judaism. In secular society, men are not expected to wear tight, revealing clothing. Men's styles are usually loose and comfortable, and keep the men well covered. Therefore, when a Jewish man wears *tzeniut* clothing, he does not look any different than any other man (except, of course, for his *kippah*). If a woman wears loose comfortable clothing that covers most of her body, then she easily stands out. (Her not showing off her body is then also taken as a sign of sexual repression and low self-esteem.) Due to this double standard in secular society, as well as one's inclination to notice only that which one considers unusual, *tzeniut* standards for women seem overemphasized with respect to standards for men.

Men are strictly forbidden from dressing in a provocative manner. They are obligated to wear clothing that not only covers them sufficiently, but also does not attract undue attention. Men are warned against beautifying themselves excessively so as not to incite the passion of women (other than their wives). Transgressing these commandments is considered a grave sin for several reasons. First of all, the man is attracting women and tempting them to sin or have obscene thoughts. Also, by attracting female attention, he is putting himself in a situation where he is tempted to sin further by flirting, becoming overly friendly with women, and ultimately engaging in relations with them. Furthermore, his actions are a reflection of a deep character flaw: pride.[1] This is true for women as well.

Pride, *ga'avah*, has a good form and a bad form. Concerning the body, there is a distinction made between vanity and being comfortable with one's body and taking good care of it. Since the body is the dwelling place of the soul, fashioned by God, it is

1   *Ways of the Tzaddikim* (Jerusalem: Feldheim Publishers, 1996), 33.

a mitzvah to take care of it.[1] Self-affliction is forbidden by the To-rah.[2] However,

> if one adorns his body in order to flaunt himself, he forgets Hashem, blessed be He, he pays no heed to the mitzvot, and he does not pursue good deeds for he is entirely intent on himself — to adorn his ephemeral body, whose end is to be devoured by worms and maggots.[3]

One often thinks that one's thoughts influence one's actions. However, the reverse is true as well. How one dresses affects how one thinks. If one dresses in a haughty fashion, he becomes haughty even if he was not so originally. In this way, he develops *ga'avah* within himself. *Ga'avah* is the antithesis of *anavah*, and *anavah* is a prerequisite to serving God.

In order to impress upon men the importance of *anavah* and *tzeniut*, the Torah gave them daily reminders. The *kippah* is worn as a constant reminder that no matter how powerful the man may think he is, there is Someone who is even more powerful than he and whom he must serve. One reason why the tallit is so big is so that the man can wrap it around himself to block out all distractions during prayer. In this way, the Torah nurtures men's external orientation by directing it to the service of God without letting it degenerate into objectification.

The Torah holds both men and women to very high standards of modesty. However, since God knows human nature, He knows that when you put men and women together, it will most likely be the men who will gawk at the women and the women who will dress immodestly to attract male attention. Therefore,

---

1   Ibid., 35–37.
2   Ibid., 35.
3   Ibid., 33.

in order to maintain a totally modest society, the Torah emphasizes modest dress for women and the guarding of one's eyes,
shemirat einayim, for men.

Men are forbidden to gaze at women who are not their
wives. Since guarding one's eyes is a very difficult commandment which a man must perform all day, he was given a special
commandment to help him: the mitzvah of tzitzit.

When a man wears a four-cornered garment (which was
common attire in ancient times), he is required to tie certain
strings in a distinct way to each corner. The details and significance of this mitzvah are beyond the scope of this book, but the
interested reader can refer to Rabbi Aryeh Kaplan's book,
Tzitzith: A Thread of Light.[1] When men no longer regularly wore
four-cornered garments, they began to wear another four-
cornered garment called a "*tallit katan*," or "small tallit," under
their shirts for the express purpose of fulfilling this mitzvah.
Men usually wear tzitzit all day long.

The root of the word *tzitzit* is "*tzutz*," which means "to
look." Every day, twice a day, men read the purpose of this
mitzvah as a part of the Shema prayer: "And it shall constitute
tzitzit for you, that you may see it and remember all the commandments of Hashem and perform them; and not explore after
your heart and after your eyes after which you stray. So that you
may remember and perform all My commandments; and be
holy to your God."[2]

Wearing tzitzit is like tying a string around one's finger in
order to remember something. Here, that "something" is remembering God's commandments and performing them. The

---

1 Found in *The Aryeh Kaplan Anthology II* (New York: Mesorah Publications,
  1998).
2 Numbers 15:39–40.

Torah does not say "that you may see [the tzitzit] and not look inappropriately at women;" rather, tzitzit are described as the key to observing all of God's commandments. One way to interpret this is that what's at stake is not just sexual immorality but the whole way of Jewish living. Sexual immorality would completely undo Jewish society. Entire civilizations have fallen due to sexual corruption.

Note that the phrase "after which you stray" is in the present tense. This tells us that this is something which is always happening. No matter how many times one has refrained from straying in the past, the threat is always there. Also, past performance is no indication of future performance. One cannot become overly confident in his ability to overcome temptation because that is precisely when he is the most vulnerable to his *yetzer hara*.

The last statement reiterates remembering and performing God's commandments. It ends with "and be holy to your God" — the purpose of the commandments and guarding oneself from straying from them.

The Torah forbids putting stumbling blocks in front of the blind.[1] In addition to the plain meaning, this means that one may not do anything that might cause a person to stumble spiritually. Although everyone is held accountable for his or her actions, people are required to help each other be a good person. In order not to put a stumbling block in front of each other, men and women are commanded to be proactively modest and not behave in a way that might lead to indecency.

---

1   Leviticus 19:14.

Tzeniut in the Woman's Path

The path given to women is difficult to observe. This is no accident, since the Torah gave women the privilege of bringing holiness to the private sphere. Since the way in which women contribute to the Jewish people is not easily seen, a person coming from a culture where visibility and importance are synonymous could logically conclude that Judaism gives women an inferior role. This would be true if importance was measured by public opinion. In Judaism, importance is measured only by God's opinion. Since God sees everything, visibility to others is irrelevant. In Judaism, the acts that are performed in complete modesty are generally the ones considered to be on the highest level of holiness.

The woman's path begins with modest dress. On a spiritual level, this allows a woman to nurture her inner orientation by deemphasizing her appearance. Although Judaism recognizes and appreciates a woman's beauty, the religious framework puts beauty in the right perspective. "Grace is false and beauty is vain, a God-fearing woman – she will be praised."[1] By emphasizing modest dress, it enforces this perspective.

A woman has a strong need to forge connections with others on a deep level. This is only possible if the other person sees her as a full human being. By not attracting attention to her external form, she helps the other person concentrate on who she is within. This is true whether the other person is a man or a woman.

Modest dress is an especially powerful weapon against the dehumanizing way contemporary society treats women. In spite

---

1   Proverbs 31:30.

of progress made in women's liberation, society still portrays women primarily as sex objects. From movies to television to advertisements to fashion, the overwhelming message is that the ideal woman is young, has a perfect body and face, and is glad to show it off to everybody.

The saddest thing is when women take this image to heart and overlook its cruelty. Numerous studies show what a debilitating effect the obsession with beauty has on women: high rates of eating disorders, depression, and low self-esteem. Even the most "liberated" women whose self-image is intact and whose self-esteem is solid feel the intense pressure. How much more so do adolescent girls, who are hit over the head with the pressure and are just forming a self-image. Dr. Mary Pipher, in her book *Reviving Ophelia*, sounded the alarm on how the pressure is destroying girls:

> Girls feel an enormous pressure to be beautiful and are aware of constant evaluations of their appearance. In an art exhibit on the theme of women and appearance, Wendy Bantam put it this way: "Every day in the life of a woman is a walking Miss America Contest."...
>
> With early adolescence, girls surrender their relaxed attitudes about their bodies and take up the burden of self-criticism. Just at the point [that] their hips are becoming rounder and they are gaining fat cells, they see magazines and movies or hear remarks by peers that suggest to them that their bodies are all wrong. Many girls scorn their true bodies and work for a false body. They allow the culture to define who they should be. They diet, exercise compulsively, and wear makeup and expensive clothes. Charlotte [one of Dr. Pipher's clients] thought of her body as

something other people would examine and judge. How her body appeared to others, not how it felt to her, was what mattered.[1]

In response to Dr. Pipher's book, Sara Shandler, who was seventeen years old at the time, organized a book with numerous contributions from teenage girls called *Ophelia Speaks*.[2] Here the Ophelias speak to the world directly, without being filtered by judging or analyzing intermediaries. Part one of the book is titled "The Body Under Assault," the topic girls wrote about the most. In the introduction to this topic, Sara Shandler writes,

> I do not have a cute nose, perfect skin, long legs, a flat stomach, or long eyelashes. My awareness of these facts makes my body a backdrop for my everyday life. My stomach, back, skin, knees, hair, are always in my peripheral vision. Never my sole focus (I'm too healthy for that!), but always just tickling at my consciousness. I sometimes catch myself comparing my body to those of actresses, models, women walking down the street. Then I remind myself: Healthy, happy, normal girls don't notice, don't envy, other women's small frames or sunken cheeks. They don't find pride in the comment, "Wow. Your collar bones really stick out." They don't feel guilty for not being as thin, or as muscular, as the star in the magazine clipping. Oh, they don't, do they? My mail tells a different story.[3]

---

1 Mary Pipher, *Reviving Ophelia: Saving the Selves of Adolescent Girls* (New York: G.P. Putnam's Sons, 1994), 55–57.

2 Sara Shandler, ed., *Ophelia Speaks: Adolescent Girls Write about Their Search for Self* (New York: Harper Perennial, 1999).

3 Ibid., 3–4.

To dress modestly is to reject this value system in the most effective way. It is like saying, "I will not be made into an object. My beauty does not come from my figure, but from within. I am beautiful regardless how close I approach some concocted ideal. It is none of anybody's business what I look like underneath my clothes. I am a human being, made in God's image, and I will not let anybody reduce me to anything less."

Some women flaunt their figures, thinking that it is sexually liberating as long as they are controlling their own sexuality instead of having others control it. The result is that instead of letting other people objectify them, they are objectifying themselves. This is not very progressive.

Furthermore, they are promoting the concept that women are primarily sex objects. Women who don't have ideal bodies may see them and feel inferior. Whether this is the intent or not is irrelevant: these are the results and women must take responsibility for them. This is especially true in a culture obsessed with beauty.

Dressing modestly, in contrast, can be seen as an affirmation of sisterhood. One goes beyond one's desires for attention and sensitizes oneself to the feelings of other women. One achieves the main goal of feminism: to always take into account the effects of one's actions on other women. One is aware of the power one has and uses it for the good.

Besides hurting other women, women who dress immodestly also hurt men. By encouraging men and boys to see them as sex objects, they hinder their maturity development. Also, these men could be husbands. They may find the women attractive and think about them, maybe even when they are with their wives. Even if they don't act on their desires, their attachment to their wives has slightly eroded. While men are held responsible for their thoughts and actions, they should be able to succeed as husbands because of other women and not in spite of them.

Every woman has a right to a husband who loves her and thinks she is the most beautiful woman in the world. This is the foundation of a happy marriage, which is the basis of a happy family, which is the cornerstone of society. Women and men are obligated to dress and act modestly so as not to at all endanger this most important relationship. Dressing modestly is especially important for women because men, being externally oriented, are much more sensitive to visual stimuli.

This is not to say that a woman should make herself look ugly, or even plain. She is allowed to wear beautiful clothes and flattering makeup and exquisite jewelry. In fact, the husband is obligated to buy his wife all these things, and a wife is warned to keep up her appearances for her husband. The key is to make oneself look attractive without being attracting.[1] For example, think of how one would dress for an interview. One would wear one's best suit and make sure one's hair, nails, and makeup were attractively done. However, one's goal would not be to attract attention to one's looks but to one's capabilities. This is exactly what dressing in a *tzeniut* manner is about: it is the art of dressing in such a way that one attracts people to one's inner qualities without blinding them by the outer qualities.

Innerness: The Essence of Jewish Living

Let us look at a deeper meaning of *tzeniut*, innerness. The essence of Judaism is found in its innerness: behind closed doors, away from human eyes, when no one else would ever

---

1 Gila Manolson, *Outside/Inside: A Fresh Look at Tzniut* (Southfield, MI: Targum Press, 1997), 51.

know the difference. This is the purest form of worship because it depends solely on one's love and fear of God, and it is uncluttered by concerns over what others might think. All acts which are at the core of Jewish living are performed in this way.

For example, on Yom Kippur, the high priest would enter the Holy of Holies completely alone to perform a service that no one else would see on which the atonement for the entire nation depended.

Parallel to the Holy of Holies in the Temple is the bedroom in the Jewish home. The union of a husband and wife is the cornerstone of society: a holy union is necessary for a holy marriage, which is needed to build a holy family, which is required in order to construct a holy nation. One of the requirements of keeping intimate relations holy is that men and women guard their sexual power so as not to profane or squander it. This is why *tzeniut* in the sense of sexual modesty is so important.

The union between husband and wife is also the way one forms all future generations. The laws which elevate this act to holiness, the laws of *taharat hamishpachah*, are carried out by the woman in complete privacy.

At the center of every prayer service is a prayer called the *Amidah*. During the *Amidah*, we speak directly to God. We pray the *Amidah* privately — speaking intently but softly so that no one else hears us, with only our lips moving. God hears us and that is enough. The intensity of prayer is not measured in how loudly we can shout or how wildly we can gesticulate, but with how much *tzeniut* we address God. We learn how to pray the *Amidah* from a woman, Hannah, when she went to pray for a child.

One of our most basic duties to others is giving *tzedakah*, charity. One of the highest forms of *tzedakah* is when neither the giver nor the receiver knows who the other is. The giver can be sure to give for only pure motives, and the receiver maintains his dignity. Once again, true greatness is found in *tzeniut*.

In addition to the above examples, we can find the value of *tzeniut* in each of our lives. We are all put in this world to perfect ourselves as human beings. This means being in a constant struggle with ourselves. The battles we rage to fix our faults and to develop our strengths generally go unnoticed. Yet, as it is written in *Pirkei Avot*, "Better is the person who can rule over his temper than the person who can capture a city."[1] The true heroes are found in our lives, not in Hollywood or storybook fantasies.

Women's being given the private role means that they have been charged with developing this private side of heroism. As it says in Psalms, "All the glory of the princess is within."[2] As wives, mothers, and mistresses of the home, women are given a unique opportunity to develop their innerness to the highest level, more so than men. Keeping a holy family, a kosher home, ushering in the Shabbat Queen, and all the acts of kindness and charity women do are pillars of Judaism, and they are done in privacy. Each of a woman's tasks are opportunities for her to develop her character, her inner beauty, and her relationship with God.

In the process, she must battle her negative traits, which her children always masterfully bring out, and unlock reserves of strength she never knew she had. She is a warrior in her own right and this is alluded to in Judaism's ode to women, "*Eishet Chayil*," "A Woman of Valor." "*Eishet*" means "a woman of."

---

1 *Avot* 4:1.
2 Psalms 45:14.

"*Chayil*" is generally translated as "valor" or "accomplishment," but it is the adjective form of *chayal*, soldier. Like a soldier, an *eishet chayil* must be strong, focused, and determined in her goals.

Since men were given the public role in Judaism, one might think that there is a double standard concerning modesty for men after all. However, acting in a public manner is only considered immodest when publicity is pursued for its own sake. Publicizing the greatness of God and of His Torah is not immodest. Even so, the Torah emphasizes that a man's greatest moments occur in private.

Before a woman is a wife or a mother, she *is*. In Judaism, a woman is not a Sleeping Beauty, sleeping in a death-like trance, waiting for her prince to kiss her and wake her up. She is quite "awake" by the time her prince comes. The "kiss" comes from the Torah, the Torah of Life. Being a wife and mother (or executive or artist or anything else, for that matter) is never a definition of who she is. However, they are expressions of who she is. Her different roles are all opportunities to actualize her potential. Being a wife and mother provide the greatest opportunity to actualize the part of her that is most God-like — her potential to give. For this reason, discussions about being a Jewish woman will always prominently feature these two roles.

Modesty can be a great aid in helping a woman develop a strong sense of self. Starting from childhood, she should be praised for her character traits (and not for how cute she looks). As she gets older, she absorbs this way of looking at herself. In a modest society, where there is no dating that is not for the sake of getting married, the girl continues to grow without the pressure of appealing to boys. Meanwhile, many girls who grow up in a secular environment are measuring their worth mostly on their popularity with the immature boys in their class. Girls who grow up in a modest society still worry about their looks, but it does not become the obsession that it is for their secular counterparts.

As the girl becomes a woman, gets married, and has children, modesty helps her maintain her sense of self. She does not have to rely on her husband or children to live vicariously through them. This allows her to be a full partner with her husband, and not just his overbearing, nagging shadow. Since she does not invest her entire ego into her children, she can be a better mother. This is because she is able to handle problems with a sense of perspective and do what is in the child's best interest, instead of viewing the child's behavior as a measure of her worth as a mother and flying into an ego-protecting rage.

Modesty is ultimately about belief in God and a constant awareness of His presence. By nurturing her innerness, the woman nurtures her relationship to God, and this serves as her lifeline through all of life's difficulties.

The primary value of *tzeniut*, innerness, pervades every aspect of Jewish living. We must dress, behave, talk, eat, laugh with *tzeniut*. The guarding of one's sexuality is one ramification of this, but *tzeniut* encompasses much more than that. *Tzeniut* is the constant awareness of the importance of that which is within. It is focusing our lives to achieving inner beauty.

As Gila Manolson writes in her book on *tzeniut*, *Outside/Inside*,

> For *tzeniut* is infinitely more than what we wear — it is a way of being emerging from a deep vision of ourselves. It is inherent in potential within every one of us, male and female, and Judaism encourages us all to nurture it. Most

crucially, it is the key to all spiritual growth and, therefore, to the health of our society. Rather than restricting, *tzeniut* is, in the most profound sense, life giving.[1]

Modesty is central to a woman's spirituality. Due to her strong inclination to forge connections, it is too easy for her to define herself through others. Modesty is the way we maintain our individual sense of self, while expressing sensitivity to the feelings of our sisters and brothers. It is the way in which we build a personal relationship with God.

Personal Reflections

The concept of *tzeniut* took me a long time to understand, and I am still learning about how to incorporate it into my life. At first, I thought *tzeniut* was about wearing nonsexy clothes. When I was in Israel, I was set up with a *chavruta* (learning partner) who was religious, and we met on a weekly basis. Out of respect for her I would wear more conservative clothes when we met. I also did this whenever I went to classes on Judaism. Dressing more conservatively meant wearing looser clothing or at least a big shirt over my tight dress. As soon as class was over, the big shirt would come off and I was back to my old way of dressing.

As I spent more time with religious people, I spent more time attired in my more modest clothing, and I realized that I was a lot more comfortable and a lot less self-conscious. When I would put back on my usual clothing, those tight jeans would feel so constricting and those revealing dresses required so much more, well, paranoia over my looks. Wearing conservative

---

1   Manolson, *Outside/Inside,* 19.

clothes required so much less work and mental energy. My growing appreciation of modest clothing grew with my growing appreciation of Judaism in general, and as time went on I wore my long skirts more and my tight jeans less. And the big shirt stayed permanently over my tight dresses.

During the winter I started to pack to go back home. I had to go through all my clothes. It was then that I realized just how far I had come. Many of my summer clothes I would never wear again. Most clothes would be wearable if they were modified. There were a couple of things, however, like my beloved black suede miniskirt, that had to go. That miniskirt made me look *great* and I had a lot of fun times wearing it. It was like an old friend. But I had to make a decision: *Is this who I am now? Is this who I want to remain?* With a sigh and with strong resolve, I threw it out.

Still, there were times even after I became religious when I felt that I just had to put on a pair of jeans or some alluring outfit. And I did. The way I see it, becoming religious is like building muscle. You have to do exercises that are just a little bit beyond your comfort level. If you do less, then you won't build muscle. If you do much more, then you will strain your muscle and make it weaker, not stronger. I became religious gradually, easing myself into my new identity and weaning myself from the old. Sometimes I regressed, but that too was part of the process. While I was wearing that pair of jeans I kept thinking about how uncomfortable they were and how I couldn't wait to get out of them. It strengthened how I felt I shouldn't dress, and therefore made me more sure of how I should. With time, these urges decreased. I'm glad I did it this way because then I knew at every step of the way that I was doing the right thing.

The final break came when I got married. I decided that I

would maintain the standards of modesty all the time. I would be a married woman and the time for games was over. I haven't worn a pair of jeans or an immodest dress in public since. And quite frankly, I haven't missed it.

The deeper meaning of *tzeniut* eluded me for a long time. When I came back to the United States and looked around me at how women were dressed and how they were portrayed by the media, I started to understand what a lack of *tzeniut* meant. The women were like mannequins: aesthetically perfect but hollow inside. Women were reduced to pretty objects. They were mute and purely ornamental. And the clothes that women wore! This never bothered me before, but it sure bothered me now. What were they thinking? What's going to happen to them in five years, ten years, when they no longer look like that? How do they expect to be taken seriously?

I realized *tzeniut* wasn't so much about how revealing your clothes are as much as what message you send with your looks. Does the way you look scream, "Look at what a pretty little thing I am"? Or does it whisper, "Now here is an interesting woman"?

Also, *tzeniut* as an expression of sisterhood became clear to me. Didn't these women who wore such provocative clothing realize how much they hurt other women who were not as young or well endowed? Did they think about how men would look at them? Of course they did, that's why they dressed like that. But it didn't seem to concern them that a lot of these men were husbands and boyfriends and they were hurting other women. Yes, the men could look away and they are held responsible if they don't, but that did not excuse these women's irresponsible behavior. I know feminists would argue that a woman should be able to wear whatever she wants. But in effect, that says that women should not be held accountable for the damage they do to other women. That sounds pretty sexist to me.

One of the last mitzvot I chose to observe was covering my hair when I got married. It just seemed so repressive, so strange. I thought I would never do it. This is where I would draw the line. But in the end, what won me over was that I suddenly perceived the beauty of it. I looked around me and observed the women I most admired and how they were building such wonderful lives. They all covered their hair. It just seemed a natural part of the total beautiful picture.

Jewish living is like a complex machine, with much assembly required. You can't just read the assembly manual, use only the parts of the machine you understand, and throw out the parts you don't. Otherwise, sooner or later, it will fall apart. I instinctively knew that covering my hair upon marriage was a necessary part in building a Jewish life.

When the time came to cover my hair, my decision caused a major upheaval in my self-image and the image I presented to others. I have beautiful hair. People often asked me if I had a perm. My hair was my best feature. It was my trademark. It was a part of my identity. Now it is tucked away in hats and snoods (a type of hair covering). Most women wear wigs. I decided not to, not because of religious reasons, but because that was and is still too strange. I just can't imagine myself wearing a wig. A big part of becoming religious is simply getting used to a different way of life. This is something I never got used to as a practice for myself, and since it is not required, I didn't force the issue.

I had to rethink who I was as a married Jewish woman and how I had changed. My look was much more adult and lost the flirtatiousness it had before. My sexuality was now channeled towards only one man. My old friends sometimes looked at me with an expression that said, "Where are you, Marina? Are you still there?" But I'm still all here. It's just that some parts of me were never meant to be visible and now they're not. That's when I learned another lesson on *tzeniut*: it means that there are some things which must be kept hidden in order to retain their preciousness.

I also became much more self-conscious in my actions because people who saw me knew that I was a religious married Jewish woman, and they expected me to behave according to the highest standards. Everything I did would reflect on Judaism and religious Jews. I heard men saying the same thing when they started to wear a yarmulke.

It wasn't till I was married that I understood what *tzeniut* meant as an expression of innerness....

Chapter 4

Family

The Akeret HaBayit — NOT a Housewife

Women were given the privilege of being the makers of Jewish homes. The Hebrew word for "homemaker" is *akeret habayit*. Before discussing what this means in the Jewish context, let us clarify what it does not mean. An *akeret habayit* is not a housewife. The woman's role at home as it was traditionally understood in American culture is very different from how it is understood in Judaism.

How men and women view women and their role at home has gone through a radical upheaval in the past thirty years. Here we will look at the traditional (i.e., pre-women's movement) housewife in America and how she contrasts with the *akeret habayit*. Even though a lot has changed in the past thirty years about how women and their roles at home are viewed, this is still a meaningful comparison for three reasons. One is that when a woman hears statements like "women were given the privilege of being the makers of Jewish homes," the image that

109

may come to mind is of this housewife. Another reason is that the image of the traditional American housewife is still very strong in American culture and has become a standard against which change is measured. Furthermore, the legal system has not kept up with social opinion, and a lot of sexist laws which are a throwback to this ideal are still operative.

The heart of this comparison is highlighting the differences between how Judaism and American culture perceive women in the context of their roles within the home.

The housewife's responsibility is seen as consisting of household chores and childcare. When much of housework became mechanized starting in the beginning of the twentieth century, the housewife found she had a lot more leisure time, and society started to emphasize her role in the emotional development of her children.

For an *akeret habayit*, housework is a means to an end, and not the end itself. *Akeret* is the feminine version of *ikar*, which is the central aspect, or the essence of something. *Bayit* usually means "house" or "home." The Temple that stood in Jerusalem was called the "Beit HaMikdash," *beit* meaning "house of" and *hamikdash* literally meaning "holiness." Often, it is referred to simply as "HaBayit," "the House." Thus, in Hebrew the same word is used for both a home and the Holy Temple. In fact, the purpose of a home is to be a *"mikdash me'at,"*[1] a miniature sanctuary.

God commanded Israel to build the sanctuary so that He could dwell *"b'tocham."*[2] *B'tocham* is often translated as "amongst them." However, its literal meaning is "within them." The purpose of a sanctuary is to help each of us build our own inner sanctuary where God can dwell. An *akeret habayit* is that

---

1   *Sotah* 17a.
2   Exodus 25:8.

central figure which transforms a home into a sanctuary where each member of her family can become a dwelling place for God's presence. Taking care of children means more than just making sure they are fed, clean, and receive quality time. It means *chinuch* – the Hebrew word for education and dedication to the service of God. We will examine the *akeret habayit*'s role in more detail in subsequent sections.

Being a housewife also meant being housebound. All of a woman's capabilities were supposed to be directed only to her home. There was no room for any self-development or pursuit of outside interests, let alone a career. To do so would seem manly and hence unnatural. It was reasoned that there is something about women, their "feminine mystique," which allows them to be fulfilled by shiny floors.

For an *akeret habayit*, there is no contradiction between valuing her central position in the home and developing her interests outside of it. A traditional Jewish woman who works outside the home considers herself every bit an *akeret habayit* as a woman who stays home. There is no "housewife" versus "career woman" dichotomy. In fact, in much of today's Orthodox society the husband studies Torah all day and the wife supports the family. In "*Eishet Chayil*," the ideal woman is described as an expert businesswoman.[1]

An *akeret habayit* is still expected to place her family above her career, but so is a man. This is due to Judaism's beliefs that the goal of a person's life, man or woman, is self-transcendence rather than self-fulfillment. Life's goal is not money, prestige, or public recognition. It is about approaching one's Creator,

---

1   Proverbs 31:16.

whether it be through creating a Jewish home or learning His will as revealed in the Torah.

In much of the non-Jewish world, part of being a married woman was being subservient and submissive to the husband. As his "helpmate" (*ezer k'negdo*), it was her job to wait on him. Here is just one example of how an idea was taken from Judaism and perverted. This was all a part of her job to "obey" her husband as he was superior to her. As John Calvin said, "Let the woman be satisfied with her state of subjection, and not take it amiss that she is made inferior to the more distinguished sex."[1] Just as the man was to subject himself to God, the woman was to subject herself to the man because he represented Godliness.

We have seen how a woman's being an *ezer k'negdo* means being in an equal relationship with her husband. A woman is considered to be made in the image of God, just like the man, and neither is seen as being more "Godly" than the other. A woman is not considered a missing piece to an otherwise whole man. She, like the man, is equal to half of the human being. In other words, a whole human being is 50 percent man and 50 percent woman, not 99 percent man and 1 percent woman, or even 51 percent man and 49 percent woman. As an *ezer k'negdo*, not only is a woman allowed to have a different opinion from her husband, but it is precisely because of her unique perspective that she is able to be his partner.

It was not enough for the housewife to be submissive to the man, she had to be subsumed by him. She was not allowed to have an independent voice. She was not allowed an independent identity. She was defined exclusively in terms of her roles as

1 Quoted in Sara Evans, *Born for Liberty: A History of Women in America* (New York: The Free Press, 1989), 22.

wife and mother. Until about 150 years ago, in American law a married woman did not have a legal identity separate from her husband. She was considered a "femme couvert," literally, "a woman under cover" of her husband.[1] This was an application of the idea that in marriage, a husband and wife are united into one entity.

This may sound like what Judaism says, but the understanding of how this unity is achieved is opposite to Judaism. The two things which distinguish the human being from animals are free will and the ability to communicate. When a woman got married, she was expected to give up both to her husband. His will was to be her will, and she was not allowed her own voice. The "unity" of husband and wife was thus achieved by stripping the woman of her humanity. This was not a unity between two human beings, but a man's acquiring a female body.

The emphasis on modesty for the Jewish woman helps her develop her identity based on her innermost self, not her familial status. Unlike a man, a woman is not obligated to marry or have children. We will examine the reason for this in a subsequent section. While there is just as much societal pressure on the woman as on the man to get married and have children, the fact that she is not obligated to do so sends a clear message that a woman is more than a wife or mother, as important as those roles are. While the ideal marriage is where the husband and wife are a single unit, the woman still retains an independent legal identity in Jewish law. She can enter into contracts, acquire and dispose of property, and be a litigant in contracts and damages.[2]

---

1 Jana B. Singer, "The Privatization of Family Law," *1992 Wisconsin Law Review*, 1462.

2 Moshe Meiselman, *Jewish Woman in Jewish Law* (New York: Ktav Publishing House, Inc., 1978), 81.

Finally, in American society, once a woman married she was at the mercy of her husband physically, sexually, and financially. A man was considered the king of his castle, where all others were his subjects. The model for this monarchy was whatever the man wanted, and many chose absolute tyranny. What went on between family members was considered a "private" affair where the courts did not want to interfere for fear of compromising the privacy of the home. Also, since a husband and wife were considered a single entity, spousal abuse was invisible as far as the law was concerned (it is legally impossible to abuse a part of one's body).

Even though a wife is no longer a "femme couvert," the belief in this unity has persisted and prevented the courts from dealing adequately with wife abuse.[1] In effect, this left wives and children with no protection against an abusive man. Even today, police protection from abusive husbands is pitiful and often nonexistent.

The Jewish courts, however, make no such distinction between public life and home life. How husbands and wives behave toward each other is well within the jurisdiction of the Jewish courts. Unlike non-Jewish courts which until recently have not even considered physical and emotional abuse a crime, Jewish courts have always been completely intolerant of such behavior. Rabbi Moses Isserles, one of the leading rabbinic authorities of post-Talmudic times, writes:

> It is a sin for a man to beat his wife, and if he does this habitually the court can punish him, excommunicate him, and whip him and apply all measures of force until he takes an oath never to do so again. If he violates this oath

---

1 Singer, "Privatization of Family Law," 1462.

he may be compelled to divorce her.[1]

Rabbi Mordechai ben Hillel, a leading rabbinic authority of the Middle Ages, writes, "As with another person whom one is commanded not to beat...even more so with one's wife, whom one is obliged to honor more than one's own self."[2] Note that both statements were written in the middle of the Dark Ages, when the rest of Europe considered beating a wife an acceptable form of husbandly discipline.

The key to the previously mentioned vulnerabilities of women is their financial dependence on their husbands. On the one hand, the woman was encouraged to withdraw from the workforce and stay home or to go into a low-paying job. She thereby became financially dependent on the man. On the other hand, the woman was not guaranteed financial security in return. In the event that her marriage became abusive, a woman's choices were often to remain and face more abuse at home, or to leave and live in abject poverty.

In American law, there is no legal minimum that the husband has to provide his wife, making it easy for him to manipulate her. Once the marriage is over, whether through divorce, the husband's death, or simply his leaving, the woman's security is further jeopardized. If the woman divorces, then her alimony and child support, assuming she gets any, often does not provide her with the same standard of living.

Under Jewish law, a man must provide for his wife's financial security both during and after the marriage, and this is enforceable by the courts. During the marriage, the minimum a man must provide for his wife is food, personal needs, clothing,

---

1   *Even HaEzer* 154:3.

2   Mordechai, *Ketubot* 185.

household needs, medical payments, and burial.[1] This severely decreases his ability to manipulate her by threatening her financial well-being. If he divorces her, he has to pay her a substantial amount of money in one lump sum which would allow her to live comfortably for at least one year.[2] This was instituted by the rabbis over two thousand years ago to prevent men from using divorce as a way to threaten or punish their wives, and to help make divorce a viable option for a woman if the situation called for it.

If a woman works, then she is still entitled to her husband's providing for all her needs. In return for this financial security, the woman's earnings belong to her husband. However, a woman can choose financial independence by stating that she wants to keep her earnings. The husband is then relieved of some of his financial obligations to her. A man, however, cannot tell his wife to work and keep her earnings so that he could lessen his responsibilities toward her.[3]

When a man dies, his widow and unmarried daughters are supported from his estate.[4] If a man has debts and he dies, then a portion of his estate must go to paying off all the debts. Whatever is left is divided among the heirs. In order to provide for the women's financial security, the widow and unmarried daughters are considered creditors. The "debt" to the widow is to provide her with financial support until she dies or remarries. She also has the right to continue living in her house. The "debt" to the unmarried daughters is their financial support until they are married. Whatever is left over is inherited by the sons. In

---

1 Meiselman, *Jewish Woman in Jewish Law*, 82.
2 Ibid., 99.
3 Ibid., 82–83.
4 Ibid., 84–95.

this way, a woman's livelihood could not be threatened by the husband either during or after marriage. At the same time, the law also helps the man to provide for a woman's financial security.

It may seem that the laws concerning financial matters between husbands and wives are unequal. However, rabbis knew that treating men and women as if they were equal (i.e., the same) in terms of financial standing would lead to vastly unequal outcomes. This has been borne out by the American experience. As Carol Tavris writes in *The Mismeasure of Woman*,

> [N]otice that at the core of this vision [of treating women "equally" to men] is our now familiar male standard of normalcy. The goal is to treat women as men already are treated....
>
> Now many scholars of legal issues are questioning the wisdom and consequences of the symmetrical vision of legal equality and focusing on the male bias at its heart. One of their most powerful arguments against symmetry is the accumulating evidence that treating women like men often produces disastrously unequal outcomes.[1]

She continues to demonstrate how treating women the same as men has left many women impoverished. The rabbis recognized that the majority of women would get married and have children and therefore be ill-equipped to financially support themselves. The Jewish laws reflect this and provide for the *akeret habayit*'s security. However, the rabbis also provided a way for married women to be financially independent. The choice between financial dependence and security, and finan-

---

1   Carol Tavris, *The Mismeasure of Woman* (New York: Simon and Schuster, 1992), 108–109.

cial independence was left to the woman.

For all the superficial similarities in the emphasis on home and family, the *akeret habayit* and the American housewife represent two different and often opposite beliefs about women, particularly married women, what their role is, and the value placed on their labor. The Jewish woman and her central role in building the Jewish family has always been highly valued in Judaism. This is reflected in Jewish values, and it is backed by the Jewish legal system.

Marriage and Mitzvah

The woman's first responsibility as the *akeret habayit* is setting the tone for her marriage. In order to appreciate the enormity of this responsibility, one must understand the importance of marriage in Judaism. Marriage is the framework through which humanity was created. All other animals were created en masse, as male and female. Only humans were created as one being, Adam, and later split into two halves, male and female. When Eve was "extracted" from the original Adam, she was brought to the new Adam to be his *ezer k'negdo*, a helpmate parallel to him. The man and woman could now only fulfill their potential through each other: the woman by helping the man and the man by letting the woman help him. When Eve is brought to Adam, he recognizes that she is "bone of my bone, flesh of my flesh."[1]

Marriage is therefore not just a relationship which is a part of one's life. Rather, it is a union which transforms two half people into one complete being. It is only after the first union oc-

---

1   Genesis 2:23.

curred that God finally called the world "very good."[1]

The reader may have noticed that the relationship between a male and female is always described as that between husband and wife. This is not a coincidence. What makes marriage different from other relationships is the degree of obligation the couple has. Obligation as a prerequisite to achieving physical, emotional, and spiritual fulfillment, love, and holiness is a reflection of a broader concept in Judaism: the concept of a mitzvah.

As discussed previously, the purpose of Judaism is to reconnect with God. The way in which one does this is through giving.

What does it mean to give? A rich man may give charity to a poor man. However, in order to show how magnanimous he is, he may publicize how he gave so much money to so-and-so. The reason he gave was in order to take honor for himself, even if it meant taking away another's dignity. His act was essentially taking.

As another example, consider a child who gives her mother a macaroni necklace that she made in school for Mother's Day. This necklace is the ugliest thing the mother ever saw. Yet what does she do? She oohs and ahhs at how beautiful it is, immediately puts it on, thanks her child, and gives her a big hug and kiss. She took the necklace, but only in order to give back love. Her act was pure giving.

Giving and taking is therefore not merely a matter of who transfers goods to whom. Both giving and taking can be a means of giving, as well as taking. The above examples illustrate how one can give in order to take and take in order to give.

Next consider the following response of someone whom a charity appeals to for a sizable contribution to be paid in Sep-

1   Ibid. 1:31.

tember: "I will give when I want, and how much I want. Who are you to tell me how much to contribute and then give me a due date?"

Everyone has a need to give. The person in the above example is stating that she will give according to her need to give, irrespective to the charity's need to receive. Satisfying this need in any way one sees fit is not truly giving to the other, it is only giving to one's self. The essence of giving is placing the receiver's needs above one's own.

In "*Eishet Chayil*," the woman "spreads out her palm to the poor, and extends her hands to the destitute."[1] To those who need a little help, she gives a little help. To those who are truly destitute, she extends both hands to help their situation. People usually prefer one type of giving to another. Some like giving a little and they don't like feeling like a sponge to those who require a lot. Others like feeling the power they have to drastically change other people's lives. True giving is when it is done according to what the other person needs, and not according to the giver's own needs.[2]

After God created Adam, He gave him one commandment: not to eat from the Tree of Knowledge of Good and Evil. God had just created the whole world for Adam's sake, and He put him in the Garden of Eden. In order for Adam not to feel like a free-loader, God gave him a commandment as an opportunity for him to give something back to God.

Another way of looking at it is that one's success in giving depends on the other person's ability to receive. God wanted Adam and Eve to have the most capacity to receive. The person

---

1 Proverbs 31:20.

2 Tzipporah Heller, *More Precious than Pearls* (Jerusalem: Feldheim Publishers, 1993), 25–26.

one can give the most of oneself to is the one who chooses to receive. God gave Adam and Eve a commandment so that they could have an opportunity to place God's will above their own. In this way, they could choose to receive God's goodness and have the greatest capability to receive from Him.

By putting God's will above their own, Adam and Eve would transform the physical world into vessels for holiness. After the sin in the Garden of Eden, the physical world became divorced from the spiritual world, and right and wrong became blurred. Elevating the physical now requires a lot more effort and discernment. God gave us the Torah which contains 613 mitzvot to teach us how to do this today.

A "mitzvah" is a commandment, but it is often translated as a good deed. Certainly it is a good deed to perform a commandment. However, the two terms have different connotations. A commandment is something one must do as a matter of course. It is expected that one fulfill it without question, regardless of one's personal feelings. A good deed connotes something one does because one feels like doing it. It is not obligatory, and one can give oneself a congratulatory pat on the back for going beyond one's duty and being so very righteous.

Obeying God's commandments means putting His will above one's own. It is giving to God according to His requirements, not ours. This is true giving, and this is what Judaism is about. If one sees religion as an institution which encourages doing only good deeds, then it becomes nothing but a vehicle for fulfilling one's own needs for giving, regardless of what God wants. It is glorified taking.

By making marriage the framework within which man and woman relate, Judaism injects obligation into their relationship. With this sense of obligation, they learn how to give. By giving, they are able to be partners with God. They attain personal ful-fillment on all levels and imbue the world with holiness.

What about love? Isn't that what marriage and our relation-ship to God is about? Love is not based on physical attraction or on how good a person or one's concept of God makes one feel. That is only self-love. The essence of the word love, *ahavah*, is giving, *hav*.[1] Love is a product of giving. It happens when one suspends one's self-centered view and concentrates on another person. By stressing mitzvah and marriage, Judaism fosters love between a person and God, and between a person and another person.

Building Shalom Bayit

The woman is uniquely qualified to set the tone for her mar-riage. Due to her extra measure of *binah*, the woman is more at-tuned to the nuances of the marriage and the relationships be-tween the children. Her need for a deep connection with her husband, coupled with her verbal strength, gives her a greater inclination to bring out problems and talk about them. The woman can therefore influence the home in a more profound manner.

Women wield an enormous power over their households. With her facial expressions, her tone of voice, and her words, a woman determines the environment of her home. It is in her hands whether it is a pleasant, loving place that encourages growth in Torah, or a dreaded residence that her children and husband long to leave. The Talmud tells us about a couple who got divorced after ten years because they had no children. Both

---

1   See Psalms 29 and Genesis 29:21.

were good people, and each married a wicked person. The man became as wicked as his new wife, while the woman's husband became as good as she.[1]

The woman must use her strengths to create *shalom bayit*, peace in the home. *Shalom*, peace, is directly related to the word *shalem*, complete. *Shalom* is therefore not merely an absence of war, nor is it simply coexistence. *Shalom* is an active state where the husband and wife work together to become *shalem*, complete. Adam and Eve were originally created as one being to teach us that only by uniting in marriage do the man and woman become one complete person. This can only be done in a marriage characterized by *shalom bayit*.

Shalom bayit is so important that God, the embodiment of absolute truth, told a lie for its sake. When the angels came to tell Abraham and Sarah that they would have a child, Sarah laughed in disbelief and exclaimed, "After I have withered shall I again have delicate skin? And my husband is old!"[2] When God told Abraham what Sarah did, He rephrased her exclamation as "Shall I in truth bear a child, though I have aged?"[3]

Ultimately, *shalom bayit* leads to *shleimut*, perfection, which is also directly related to *shalom* and *shalem*. God's presence, the *Shechinah*, only dwells with a couple when they have *shalom bayit*.[4]

The *Shechinah* is not considered simply a nice addition to a home, it is an absolutely vital part. A Jewish marriage is not a partnership of two but of three: man, woman, and God. This can be seen by the Hebrew words for man and woman. A man is *ish*,

---

1   *Bereishit Rabbah* 17:12.
2   Genesis 18:12.
3   Ibid., 14.
4   *Sotah* 17a.

spelled *alef-yud-shin*, and a woman is *ishah*, spelled *alef-shin-hei*. The letters *alef* and *shin* are common to both. *Alef-shin* spells *eish*, which means fire. *Ish* has the letter *yud* and *ishah* has the letter *hei*. *Yud-hei* spells God's name. When the woman and man come together, they can utilize their fire to connect with God and make Him their partner. Without God between them, all they have left is a consuming fire (*eish*) which will destroy them.[1]

How does the couple build *shalom bayit* and make God a partner? Essentially, by fulfilling the commandments. For example, when each gives the other the benefit of the doubt, he or she fulfills the commandment to judge your fellow favorably. When both are careful in their conversations not to gossip, they fulfill the prohibition against being "a talebearer among your people." When each goes out of their way to do nice things for the other, they are fulfilling the commandment to "love your neighbor as yourself."

Applications to Everyday Living

The Jewish homemaker's goal is to make her home a *mikdash me'at*. Practically, this means building and maintaining *shalom bayit* (peace in the home), the proper environment necessary to create a Torah home. Against this backdrop she develops her potential, helps her husband develop his, raises children to be good Jews, and monitors the health of the relationships among the family members. In addition, she provides for her family's physical needs.

Somehow these lofty goals get buried underneath the piles

---

1   *Sotah* 17b.

of laundry and dirty dishes over the course of the day. The woman performs the mundane household tasks only to see, almost immediately, all her work undone. There seems to be no end to the floors that need to be washed, the diapers that need to be changed, the meals that need to be cooked. Any sense of accomplishment is fleeting as little hands and feet quickly run to undo all her efforts. The repetitiveness of mundane tasks and the lack of a tangible, measurable achievement make the homemaker feel like she is living a life of futility.

One way to combat this is to appreciate the importance of the everyday chores that one does. If the *akeret habayit* dresses her toddler, she performed a mitzvah. If two minutes later the toddler gets his clothes dirty and needs to be dressed again, the mother can perform another mitzvah. A mitzvah is indestructible and it cannot be taken away. Even if in this world one's work can be undone, on another level it is eternal.

One way to see this is as follows. Imagine that one is placed in a room filled with treasures. In order to be able to keep one of these precious treasures, one has to physically carry it to a storage place outside. However, this wealth that one gathers will not be available for use until some time later. One does not know how long one has to wait, but the longer one waits the more riches one can collect. Also, one does not know the relative value of the objects, only their perceived size. Therefore, a large gem may not be anywhere near the value of a tiny gem, for example if the former was an amethyst and the latter was a diamond. What would one do? Surely one would collect as much as possible, giving equal attention to the larger jewels as to the smaller ones.

Mitzvot are our treasures, and the world is our treasure room. We are urged to "take" as many mitzvot as we can. Even though we do not always benefit from them right away, we are confident that in the end we will get our reward. Furthermore, as it says in *Pirkei Avot*, "One should be as careful in the performance of a simple commandment as in the performance of a difficult one, for one never knows the reward given for respective commandments."[1] We cannot rely on our own perceptions of what the "important" mitzvot are, so we cannot discount the "small" mitzvot. This is a good thing to remember when one is washing what seems like the thousandth dish for the day.

Another way to keep one's goals from being lost in the ordinariness of everyday life is to realize how important every interaction is, particularly to a child, and to weave Torah ideals into one's everyday conversation. Compare the following excerpt from Sarah Chana Radcliffe's *Aizer K'negdo* which shows contrasting conversations and their effects on the home.

Wrong:

Wife (to husband): "Every time I ask you to do something for me you're too busy! You never help me out at all!"

Right:

Wife (to husband): "I asked you to take out the garbage twice this week and you didn't do it. I had to do it myself. What can we do to avoid this happening in the future?"[2]

In the "wrong" example, the wife is setting the stage for a fight. The words *every time* and *never* are rarely true; there probably have been occasions when the husband has helped her. Also, implicit in her statement are the accusations: "You are selfish!" "You are inconsiderate!" "You don't love me!" The problem

---

1   *Avot* 2:1.

2   Sarah Chana Radcliffe, *Aizer K'negdo* (Southfield, MI: Targum Press, 1988), 136.

becomes her husband, not the lack of his help. The husband now feels that he has to defend himself against his accuser, and he will probably add a few choice remarks about her character traits. The wife's need for help will not be addressed, feelings will be hurt, and the marriage will suffer.

In the "right" example, the wife states a specific problem and asks her husband to work with her on a solution. There are no accusations, no embellishments, just a concrete and solvable problem. The husband does not feel like he has to defend himself but instead is guided to help deal with the issue at hand. The message the wife sends is "I am confident that we can work this out." Her needs will be addressed, and this will become an opportunity to strengthen the marital relationship.

Or, consider what happens when a child interrupts her mother's working by asking for help unzipping her coat. As Sarah Chana Radcliffe writes in *Akeres Habayis*,

> ...Mother can put down her mop for a moment, go give [the child] the help, a warm hug, a smile, a few kind words, and then return to her [washing the] floor. It's so easy and so much more beneficial than what frustrated moms have been known to do: angrily put the mop aside, hurriedly unzip the coat while berating the child for the interruption, and quickly get back to work.[1]

In the latter scenario, the mother is impatient and makes the child feel like she is not as important as a clean floor. In the former scenario, the mother infuses her home with love, patience, and loving kindness — hallmarks of a Torah home.

The work that the *akeret habayit* does around the house is

---

1 Sarah Chana Radcliffe, *Akeres Habayis* (Southfield, MI: Targum Press, 1991), 69

avodah. Avodah has two meanings, physical labor and prayer. This can be interpreted two ways. Prayer, our direct communication with God, is hard work. It is not something one can expect to do effortlessly. It requires discipline, concentration, practice, and a desire to come close to God. Another interpretation is that physical labor, when properly directed, can be a form of prayer. The greater the effort and the more one directs one's work to God, the closer one comes to Him.

For example, consider some of the daily activities of the *kohanim*, the priests who served in the Temple:

> Every morning, a lot was cast among the *kohanim* to determine who would fulfill the daily service of removing a handful of ashes from the altar. This was the first mitzvah of the day.... The *kohein* [singular of *kohanim*] singled out by lot...would ascend the altar, take a handful of ashes from it, and place them in the silver pan. He had to carry the pan with the ashes to the east side of the ramp and deposit them on the ground in a special spot designated for this purpose.... [Then] all the *kohanim* who were on duty that day...hurried up to the *mizbe'ach* to clear it of the remaining ashes. They piled them up in the center of the altar in a heap....[1]
>
> Hashem commanded that the *kohanim* arrange three different stacks of wood...on the altar.[2]
>
> He [the *kohein*] prepared [the daily offering] by mixing oil and flour, breaking the dough into pieces the size of a *kezayis* [olive] each, salting them, and burning them on the

---

1   M. Weissman, ed., *The Midrash Says: The Book of Vayikra* (New York: Benei Yaakov Publications, 1982), 45.
2   Ibid., 47.

altar together with a handful of incense.[1]

The *kohanim* had to refill the lamps of the menorah every evening.[2]

Taking out ashes, piling wood, mixing oil and flour, lighting lamps – these are all things that anyone, even a child, could have done. However, only a *kohen* could make this work an *avodah*, a service to God. Likewise, while anyone could come and clean the house, it is the *akeret habayit* who transforms the labor into *avodah* and transforms her home into a temple.

The above does not mean that all the housework must fall on the woman. How it is allocated between herself, her husband, her children, and hired help will depend on the circumstances and on preferences. However, neither should this "labor" be looked down upon as beneath oneself – for it can be made into a labor of love.

Taharah and Tumah – Philosophical and Mystical Insights

The most powerful way to make God an integral part of the marriage relationship is by following the laws of *taharat hamishpachah*. In summary, these laws state that during menstruation (or for a minimum of five days from the onset of menstruation, whichever is longer) and for seven days afterwards, a woman has the status of *niddah*, during which time she may not have relations with her husband. [This is a simplified explanation, given only for the purposes of this discussion. For a full

---

1   Ibid., 52.
2   Ibid.

treatment of the laws of *taharat hamishpachah*, I recommend *The Secret of Jewish Femininity* by Tehilla Abramov.[1] *Total Immersion* by Rivkah Slonim[2] is an enlightening compilation of essays exploring *mikveh* on a religious, historical, and personal level.] There are other restrictions having to do with the Temple. However since there is no Temple today, these restrictions currently do not apply. After the seven days, she immerses in a *mikveh*, a special collection of waters, and becomes *tahor*, ritually pure. She may then resume relations with her husband.

The laws of *taharat hamishpachah* are perhaps the least understood and the most vilified area of Jewish life. For a woman to have a distinct status when she is menstruating that separates her from certain areas of life brings to mind the most primitive customs where menstruating women were placed in entirely different huts and cut off from the rest of the tribe. This ugly vestige of primitive misogyny certainly has no place in any modern, enlightened religion. Yet a study of the laws of *taharat hamishpachah* shows that one cannot equate these laws to those of primitive cultures. Instead what one finds is a system that brings a rhythm to living that is especially relevant to modern life and is surprisingly enlightened.

Misconceptions

Translating is a tricky science. Not only does one have to know the meanings of all the words, but one also needs to understand a language's idioms. But languages are not merely collections of words, and translating is not a simple function of

---

1   Tehilla Abramov and Malka Touger, *The Secret of Jewish Femininity* (Southfield, MI: Targum Press, 1988).

2   Rivkah Slonim, *Total Immersion: A Mikveh Anthology* (Northvale, NJ: Jason Aronson, Inc., 1993).

mapping one word to another. Language develops in the context of the culture it is in. By culture, I mean the totality of beliefs and points of view of that group of people. Language is therefore a representative of culture. In order to translate, it is not enough to be linguistically fluent in a foreign language. One must also completely understand the culture from which the language came.

Even when cultures are similar, their slight differences result in words that mean the same thing having different connotations. This is why jokes are usually not funny in translation. When the cultures are very different, then often there are words that are untranslatable. These are usually the words that represent concepts which are foreign to the other culture. What should a translator do? One option is to use the closest approximation one can, regardless of its inappropriateness. The other option is to transliterate the original word, and describe what it represents in an appendix. Neither option is very satisfactory; however, the latter is more accurate.

This problem with translation is the source of many misunderstandings of Judaism. *Taharah* and *tumah* are generally translated as "purity" and "impurity." This is very misleading, since *purity* connotes goodness, cleanliness, and innocence, while *impurity* connotes sin, filth, and licentiousness. These connotations have no place in the Jewish context.

Many mitzvot, commandments from God, require one to become *tamei* (the adjective form of *tumah*). One becomes *tamei* when coming in contact with a dead body. Yet burying the dead is an important mitzvah that is described as an act of true loving kindness. A man and woman become *tamei* when they have relations, and a woman is *tamei* after giving birth. Yet the first commandment was to procreate. There is also a separate obligation for a husband to have relations with his wife. Surely God would not command us to be sinful, filthy, or lewd.

Some interpret a woman's being a *niddah* as resulting from Judaism considering her more sinful or somehow dirty during menstruation. First of all, there is no concept in Judaism of original sin. A person is born completely innocent. God gave everyone a good inclination and an evil inclination and free will. It is only when one uses her free will to follow her evil inclination that one commits a sin. Sin is not a state one is put into; it is something one must actively choose. Also, if being *tamei* was considered sinful, then one could argue that a person automatically becomes sinful when she dies. Obviously this is not the case for death, the ultimate *tumah*. How much more so is this not true for the *niddah*, a lesser degree of *tumah*.

Secondly, being a *niddah* has nothing to do with dirt or cleanliness. Before immersing in a *mikveh*, a woman is 100 percent clean. Yet her status is exactly the same as when her menstruation started. The goal of the immersion is to recreate the birth experience. In order to do this, one must be in the same natural state, free of any foreign object, that one was the first time one was born. Therefore, even things which are not considered dirt, such as fake nails or jewelry, must be removed. Only immersion in a *mikveh* makes her *tahor*.

There are some who hold that the laws concerning a *niddah* are only ancient hygiene practices. These are the same people who say that the reason pork is prohibited is because of the risk that trichinosis once posed. It is true that there are enormous health benefits from living a life of Torah. Many researchers believe that adhering to the laws of *taharat hamishpachah* helps prevent cervical cancer.[1] A study in 1967 showed that the rate of cervical cancer among Jewish women with respect to non-Jewish women increased from 1/20 to 1/5 over the preceding fifty years. Since the rate among non-Jewish women has remained constant over that period, this means that the rate of cervical cancer among Jewish women quadrupled.[2] It was then noted that over this period, the observance of the laws of *taharat hamishpachah* among Jewish women declined dramatically.[3]

The health benefits should not be surprising since the One who wrote the Torah is the same One who created us. But there is a difference between the benefits one receives from actions and the reasons for doing those actions. The benefits of Jewish living are infinite. Some we are able to appreciate, and others we may not even realize. However, there is ultimately only one reason for observing the commandments: because God said so.

Taharah and Tumah

The laws of *taharat hamishpachah* are one application of more general concepts in Judaism: *taharah* and *tumah*. I cannot explain these concepts; nobody can. They are decrees from God, *chukim*, for which no reason is given. Our observance of *chukim* are based on our faith in God and our obligation to fulfill His commandments. They are beyond human intelligence and rules of logic, and therefore our observance of them is not dependent on our understanding. Still, it is nice when we are able to appreciate the benefits from observing them, or when we are able to

---

1   A. Baram and A. Schachter, *The Lancet* (Nov. 27, 1982), 747; R. Stein-Werblowsky, ibid., 1213; D. Skegg, P. Corwin, C. Paul, ibid. (Sept. 11, 1982), 581–583.

2   K. T. Abu-Daoud. 1967 *Cancer* 20:1706.

3   A. Singer, et al., 1968, Editorial, *Medical Journal of Australia*, 1138.

have a glimpse of their wisdom. Here we will look at some interpretations of these concepts and try to appreciate their beauty.[1]

Judaism is a religion that is based on life. There is a belief that there will ultimately be a revival of the dead and a world to come. But our job is to concentrate on this world and make the most out of the life we currently have.

The purpose of life is to fully actualize the soul's potential. In order to do this, a soul needs to be in a living body that can observe the commandments. A soul by itself cannot give charity, pray to God, act kindly to others, or observe Shabbat. Without the action that a body allows, a soul remains static; it cannot ascend closer to God. Since life is so central to Judaism, the Torah is sensitive to all its different nuances. Life and death become a spectrum, and the Torah precisely defines every point on this spectrum.

A body can be seen as a tunnel which allows the soul to ascend. Depending on how much life is in the body, this tunnel can contract and expand, thereby varying one's potential for spiritual growth. When this tunnel is contracted, one is in a state of *tumah*. The degree of *tumah* depends on the degree of the contraction. When the tunnel is at its normal or expanded state, this is *taharah*.

A person is born *tahor*. There are a number of ways that one becomes *tamei*, all of which are in some way related to death. Judaism recognizes that one's life has two parts — one's own life, and one's potential to create new life. When either part dies, one becomes *tamei*.

When a man has a seminal emission[2] or when a woman

---

1 The following explanation is based on Aryeh Kaplan's *Waters of Eden* (New York: Union of Orthodox Jewish Congregations of America, 1982).

2 Leviticus 15:16.

menstruates, he or she is *tamei*.[1] A woman also becomes *tamei* when she gives birth.[2] Although for the baby there is an abundance of life, the woman herself has lost life. The amount of life she lost depends on the gender of the baby. Females have more life potential due to their ability to bear children; therefore, the birth of a girl means the mother has lost more life. We now know that girls are born with all their eggs, albeit in immature form, while boys do not develop sperm until preadolescence. Therefore, a woman remains *tamei* for a minimum of two weeks if she gives birth to a girl,[3] and a minimum of one week if she gives birth to a boy.[4] When a person dies, the tunnel is completely cut off. Death is therefore the ultimate state of *tumah*.[5]

Anyone who is *tamei* is forbidden to go to the Temple grounds. A woman who is a *niddah* is also prohibited from having relations with her husband.[6] Since the Temple does not stand today, we are no longer concerned about other forms of *tumah* and many of the restrictions of the *niddah*. When the Temple will be rebuilt, these laws will once again be relevant. The only applicable part of these laws today are those concerning the *niddah* and her relationship with her husband.

A woman becomes a *niddah* when blood comes from her uterus or when her uterus opens. The root of the word *niddah* is *nadad*, meaning separate. This alludes to her separating from intimate contact with her husband.

Since one becomes *tamei* through death, in order to become *tahor* again one needs rebirth. The exact way in which one be-

1 Ibid., 19.
2 Ibid. 12:2–5.
3 Ibid., 5.
4 Ibid., 2.
5 Kaplan, *Waters of Eden*, 77.
6 Leviticus 15:19.

comes *tahor* (the adjective form of *taharah*) depends on how one got *tamei*, and a full discussion is beyond the scope of this book. The key part of becoming *tahor* is immersing in a *mikveh*.

Mikveh

A *mikveh* is a small pool which contains at least forty *se'ah* (two hundred gallons) of rainwater[1] that was collected naturally, according to very specific laws. If it is to be inside a building then it must be built directly into that building. Anything which can be disconnected from the building, such as a bathtub, can never be a *mikveh*. In man-made *mikveh*s, there are usually at least two pools which are separated by a wall. There is a hole in the wall which is at least two inches in diameter so that the water can flow freely between the pools. One of these pools is where the water is naturally collected. This is the original *mikveh*. The other pools are where women actually immerse. These are filtered, purified, and kept at a comfortable temperature. Since the water can flow freely between the *mikveh* and the immersion pools, the immersion pools are granted the legal status of a *mikveh*.

Why does a person need to immerse in a *mikveh* as part of the process of becoming *tahor*? What is it about the *mikveh* that gives it such power?

After one has experienced death and became *tamei*, one needs to be "reborn" to his original *tahor* status.[2] The *mikveh* is the womb through which this rebirth takes place.[3] The *mikveh* is the perfect womb[4] because once water has the status of a *mikveh*,

---

1 Kaplan, *Waters of Eden*, 5.
2 Ibid., 35.
3 Ibid., 45.
4 Ibid., 70.

it cannot be made *tamei*.[1] Because of its irreversible status as *tahor*, the *mikveh* represents Man before the sin.[2]

In the Talmud, the womb is compared to a grave.[3] How can the place of the origin of life be equated with the place of the end of life? Instead of seeing life as a line segment with the womb and the grave as the endpoints, imagine that this line is bent into the shape of a circle. Now, the womb and the grave are on the same exact point!

Judaism sees life and death as nodes on a cycle. Death is not considered the end. There is a parable about two twins who grew up together in the womb. One day, they see a great light and one of the twins is born at that moment. The other twin mourns because his brother "died."[4] Death is but a phase for the next stage of life, just like the nine-month period a fetus spends in the womb.

We can now see why a womb is like a grave and what these have in common with a *mikveh*. Say one is currently in life stage A. When a person leaves stage A, the tunnel through which that person goes through is called a grave. When that person comes out at the other end of the tunnel at life stage B, this same tunnel is called a womb. The grave and the womb are therefore two sides of the same tunnel — the terminology depends on one's point of view. The *mikveh*, the womb, and the grave are all the same in that they are the vehicles through which one changes one's status.

The structure of the *mikveh* is intimately connected to the womb and to birth. The *mikveh* must have at least forty *se'ah* of

---

1 Ibid., 56.

2 Ibid., 35.

3 *Berachot* 15b.

4 Y. Tucazinsky, *Gesher HaChaim* (Jerusalem: Etz Chaim Publications, 1993) 28.

water. Forty is a number that occurs numerous times in the Torah, always in association with birth. For example, it takes forty days from conception for an embryo to have the status of a fetus. We now know that this is when the embryo takes on a human form. Also, when the Torah was transmitted to Moses, it was "born" into this world. Therefore, this process took forty days.[1]

The physical act of immersion recreates the experience of birth. First, one must be perfectly clean — no foreign substance may come between one's body and the water. Then, when one immerses, one must be completely submerged in the water — not even a single hair is allowed to float on the surface. One is like a fetus, just about to be born. When one emerges from the *mikveh*, one is likewise reborn anew, in one's original *tahor* state.

But immersion in a *mikveh* accomplishes much more than this. It allows a person to connect with God, the ultimate source of life, and reestablish her link to Eden.[2]

> Hashem God planted a garden in Eden, to the east, and placed there the man whom He had formed. And Hashem God caused to sprout from the ground every tree that was pleasing to the sight and good for food; also the Tree of Life in the midst of the garden, and the Tree of Knowledge of Good and Evil.
>
> A river issues forth from Eden to water the garden, and from there it is divided and becomes four headwaters. The name of the first is Pishon, the one that encircles the whole land of Havilah, where the gold is. The gold of that land is good; *bedolach* is there, and the *shoham* stone. The

---

1   Kaplan, *Waters of Eden*, 68–69.
2   Ibid., 35.

name of the second river is Gihon, the one that encircles the whole land of Kush. The name of the third river is Hidikel, the one that flows toward the east of Assyria; and the fourth river is the Euphrates.

Hashem God took the man and placed him in the Garden of Eden, to work it and to guard it. And Hashem God commanded the man saying, 'Of every tree of the garden you may freely eat; but of the Tree of Knowledge of Good and Evil, you must not eat thereof; for on the day you eat it, you shall surely die."[1]

The story of Genesis tells us about Man and his condition before and after the sin. In the middle, this story seems to be interrupted by a detailed account of the rivers that went out of Eden. The Talmud tells us that these rivers are both the physical and the spiritual source of all the water in the world.[2] This is why only rainwater collected naturally can be a *mikveh*. Even though no one can reenter the Garden of Eden today, one can reestablish one's link with Eden by associating oneself with these rivers.[3] The Midrash tells us that this is what Adam did when he was driven out from Eden — he repented by sitting in a river.[4] In this way, he was trying to maintain a link with Eden. Therefore, when a person immerses in a *mikveh*, he is also reestablishing a link with Eden and with Man's perfected state. Only then can he enter the Holy Temple. Only then can a *niddah* participate in the holy act of cohabitation.

---

1 Genesis 2:8–17.
2 *Bechorot* 55a, see Malbim on Genesis 2:10.
3 Aryeh Kaplan, *Waters of Eden*, 35.
4 *Pirkei DeRabbi Eliezer* 20 (47b).

Some Misgivings

Even without the misunderstandings, a woman can be quite uncomfortable being told that she has a certain status as a result of her menstruation. Part of this is a result of the way menstruation is viewed in society.

In the past, menstruation was viewed with acute shame. The monthly cycle was thought to dominate women to the point of making them too unstable for decision-making positions. Today, the shame is still there. There may be a lot more openness about it, but a girl or woman still only leaves the drugstore with feminine hygiene products if they are in opaque bags. Currently, menstruation is considered an inconvenience that can happily be overcome with the proper medication and feminine hygiene products. The very term "feminine hygiene" is a clear indication of how the menstrual flow is viewed.

Judaism takes neither of these approaches. Certainly this is a private part of a woman's life and her privacy should be respected. A woman's monthly cycle does not control her; that would go against the fundamental belief of free will. However, it does influence her on every level. At the time of their period, women often need more solitude, more time for quiet reflection.

The Torah is sensitive to a woman's needs and provides a structure where her needs are met. By prohibiting intimate relations, the Torah forces a husband and wife to show their affection in nonphysical ways.

With physical contact forbidden, a woman finds the time to be more reflective and thoughtful. What is there to reflect about? A life could have developed this month, but instead it died. Every month, every moment is so precious. We have to take care not to let it go to waste but live every moment to our potential. One reason why women are not obligated in most time-bound commandments is because these commandments were designed to teach about the sanctity of time, and women already understand this concept completely and intimately through their monthly cycles.[1]

Instead of ignoring the topic or treating it with horror, Judaism shows women how to use their monthly cycles as an opportunity to learn about God and draw closer to Him.

Another reason a woman can be uncomfortable with the concept of *niddah* is because of the idea that she should be restricted from something simply because she has menstruated. What is so wrong about intimacy without immersion? And why should she have been prohibited from going to the Temple grounds?

When Adam and Eve were created, they only had an internal inclination toward goodness. The evil inclination was external, embodied in the snake. What was right and wrong was clear. Had they attached themselves to God, the source of all life, they could have remained immortal.[2]

Instead, Adam and Eve replaced their judgment of right and wrong over God's and violated His commandment not to eat of the Tree of Knowledge of Good and Evil. The evil inclination became an intrinsic part of them. Right and wrong became blurred, and Man was to be constantly tempted and frustrated by the inner conflict that raged within him. They distanced themselves from God, the source of life. The result was *tumah*, of which death is a consequence.[3] It is like when one is in a dark room where a single candle provides all the light. When one moves away from the light, the result is that one is in darkness.

---

1   Norman Lamm, *A Hedge of Roses* (Jerusalem: Feldheim Publishers, 1977), 76–78.
2   Kaplan, *Waters of Eden*, 33.
3   Ibid.

The darkness is not a thing one goes to, but the result of one's distancing oneself from the light. Likewise, *tumah* is the spiritual darkness which resulted when Adam and Eve distanced themselves from the light of God.

Ever since, the goal of Mankind has been to return to Eden, to return to the idyllic state before sin and death. The first ten generations degenerated into evil until they were wiped out by the flood. The next ten generations degenerated likewise, until Abraham. Abraham was able to perceive God as the only God, and he yearned to attach himself to Him. His realization became a way of life for his family. When this family became a nation, they accepted this way of life as their mission in an oath at Mount Sinai.

God taught the Jews how to recreate Eden by instructing them on how to build the sanctuary in the desert, and then the Temple in Jerusalem. These places were to be completely consecrated to God, free from *tumah*. This is why anyone who was *tamei*, man or woman, was forbidden to enter the Temple under the severest penalty.[1]

The home is a miniature temple, and the bedroom is analogous to the Holy of Holies, the innermost sacred chamber in the Temple where the two tablets from Sinai were. When done according to the laws of Torah and not perverted, intimacy is the holiest union between a man and woman and is associated with the state before expulsion from Eden. Menstruation is a cycle of death and rebirth that is a direct result of the sin in Eden. (Be careful with the logic here. The sin in the Garden of Eden caused *tumah*, death is a consequence of *tumah*, and menstruation is one form of death. This does not mean that death or menstruation or being in a state of *tumah* causes one to become sinful or

1 Ibid., 34.

are the result of an individual's sins.) Menstruation is one result of the state after expulsion from Eden. A woman needs to first go to the *mikveh*, the womb in its perfected state, and reconnect to Eden. Only then can she and her husband join God and draw down the holiest souls into this world.[1]

Taharat HaMishpachah: The Secret of a Happy Jewish Marriage

The laws of *taharat hamishpachah*, while beyond human logic, masterfully bring out the best in a marriage. The Torah wants a man and woman to be together, and this system enhances intimacy on all levels. Every month the couple relives the wonder of their first night together. Even holding hands gains appreciation, and a hug is not taken for granted.

By following these laws, the relationship gets a rhythm which allows all of its parts to develop and none to overpower the others. In the beginning of the marriage, desire is not allowed to stifle all other aspects of the relationship. This helps the couple achieve a more multidimensional union. As the husband and wife get older, the demands of work, children, and elderly parents may sap their energy and desire. The cycle of *taharat hamishpachah* helps the couple regularly refocus on each other and reignite their passion.

The laws of *taharat hamishpachah* create a framework which helps the couple to develop good communication skills outside the physical realm, thus allowing the relationship to de-

---

1   Ibid., 40–46.

velop in all its richness. When the couple cannot be physically intimate, they still desire to communicate and interact. This desire inspires them to look to other ways of showing their feelings. The temporary celibacy of *taharat hamishpachah* motivates the couple to develop all aspects of their marriage to a degree they otherwise would not.

Jewish mysticism speaks of two types of love, *ahavah shel eish*, love that is like fire, and *ahavah shel mayim*, love that is like water. As Rivkah Slonim says in the introduction to her book, *Total Immersion*,

> [*Ahavah shel eish*] is hot and passionate; it abates and flares-up cyclically in its quest to rise ever higher. This flaming emotion must be guarded lest it sputter and die. [*Ahavah shel mayim*] is cool, deep, and ever present; it is not extinguishable, there is no fear of an eclipse.[1]

A marriage needs a balance of both water and fire: too much fire will make the water evaporate and too much water will put out the fire. Living according to the laws of *taharat hamishpachah* helps a couple achieve this balance.

By observing the laws of *taharat hamishpachah*, the couple elevates the entire family to the holiest level. Everything from the everyday routines to the most intimate moments is made to transcend the emotional and physical spheres and become a worship of God. It is a sign of God's utmost trust in the woman that He placed the observance of these laws almost entirely in her hands.[2] As the guardian of the family's *taharah*, the *akeret habayit* holds the key to the family's holiness and therefore the

---

1   Rivkah Slonim, *Total Immersion*, xxxiv–xxxv.
2   She obviously cannot be held responsible for the laws that apply to her husband (e.g., touching her).

key to the holiness of the Jewish people. She therefore has the unique capability of making her home a true *mikdash me'at*.

Women and Sexuality

The Torah encourages both husbands and wives to develop the best possible intimate relationship. The Torah is also very sensitive to the woman's more complex needs and how easily they may be overlooked. The Torah pays particular attention to the woman's sexuality and strongly admonishes the husband to satisfy her needs on every level.

Jewish law obligates the husband to fulfill his wife's sexual needs.[1] The name for this mitzvah is *onah*. How a man is expected to fulfill this mitzvah can be understood from the literal meaning of *onah*, which means "a response to her." This implies that the physical act is not sufficient to fulfill this mitzvah. The husband must do so in a way that is appealing to her on an emotional, psychological, spiritual, and physical level. The *Iggeret HaKodesh* writes:

> Therefore you should begin with words that will draw her heart to you and will settle her mind and will make her happy to unite your mind with her mind and your intention with her intention. Tell her things, some of which will produce in her desire, attachment, love, willingness. Tell her words which will draw her to fear of Heaven and to piety and modesty (*tzeniut*).... Do not hasten to arouse her desire, so that her mind will be at peace. Begin in a pleasing manner of love so that she will be satisfied first [i.e., the woman should achieve satisfaction before the man].[2]

---

1   Rambam, *Hilchot Ishut*, ch. 12.
2   *Iggeret HaKodesh*, quoted in *Kitvei HaRamban*, ed. Chavel, 2:336.

He is obligated not only concerning the quality of their relations but also the quantity. The Rabbis specified the husband's minimal obligation depending on his occupation.[1] Furthermore, a husband needs his wife's permission to go away for a long time (i.e., for a business trip) or to change to a profession which would lessen the amount of time he could be with her. In addition to these minimum number of times, he has to be with her whenever he senses she wants to be with him. If he wants to be with her, then she should only be with him if she is willing. He is forbidden from being with her against her will.

The woman has no parallel obligation to her husband. Note that this commandment is entirely different from the commandment to have children. Therefore, the husband must fulfill it even when there is no chance of pregnancy, such as when a woman is already pregnant, is past menopause, or is infertile.

In addition to a positive commandment on the man to satisfy his wife, there is a negative commandment incumbent on both the husband and wife not to withhold sex from each other. If one is considering divorce, then intimate relations are forbidden. Similarly, if the couple had an argument then they shouldn't be together until they have made peace. However, neither can use sex as a weapon to punish the other or to assert their power.

The Path to Redemption

Living a traditional Jewish lifestyle teaches women how to harness their sexuality and use it in a constructive manner. Many of the women whom Judaism considers the greatest heroines are known for how they mastered their sexuality and used it for good. A few examples are Yehudit, Yael, Queen Esther,

---

1   Rambam, *Hilchot Ishut*, 14:1–2.

Tamar, and Ruth. Let us examine how each of these women used their unique feminine potential to pave the road for Redemption.

Yehudit[1] and Yael[2] each saved the Jewish people in times of war by seducing the enemy generals and then killing them when they fell asleep. Queen Esther saved the Jews from annihilation by using her charm to influence the king.[3] We celebrate this event every year during the holiday of Purim.

In order to understand the stories of Tamar and Ruth, one must understand the laws of levirate marriage. If a married man dies and leaves no offspring, his brother must either marry his widow and father children in the man's name or perform a ceremony releasing himself from this obligation. (Today the only option is to perform the ceremony.) In ancient times, the closest male relative, even if he wasn't the brother of the deceased, also had the option of marrying the widow.

Judah, the son of Jacob and the head of one of the most prominent tribes of Israel, married his oldest son to Tamar. Since his son did not want to mar Tamar's beauty by impregnating her, he "spilled his seed." For this he was immediately punished by God and he died. Tamar then married the second son, who suffered a similar fate. She was then to marry the third son, but he was still too young. As time passed and Tamar saw that no arrangements were being made for the wedding, she took matters into her own hands. She heard that Judah would be passing through her town, and so she disguised herself and enticed him to be with her. She became pregnant, and when Judah realized what Tamar had done, he exclaimed that she was more

---

1   Book of Maccabees.
2   *Nazir* 23b.
3   Book of Esther.

righteous than he.[1] Indeed, Tamar is praised by the Sages for her conduct.

Ruth was a Moabite princess who married a Jewish man. This man came to Moab with his parents and his brother when there was a famine in Israel. His brother also married a Moabite. The father and two sons died, and the mother, Naomi, decided to return to her relatives in Israel. She urged her two daughters-in-law to go back to their fathers' homes, but Ruth refused to go. Instead she answered, "Where you will go, I will go, and where you stay, I will stay. Your people shall be my people, and your God my God."[2]

Naomi's husband had lost all their wealth in Moab, and so Naomi and Ruth came to Israel penniless. Ruth took it upon herself to provide for the two of them. She went to glean in the fields of Boaz, a distant relative of Naomi, as was the custom of the poor. Boaz noted her modesty and treated her kindly. When Ruth told this to Naomi, she advised her to take the initiative. Ruth was to go to Boaz at night at the threshing floor, where he slept during the harvest season, and tell him he was her next of kin (and therefore obligated to marry her according to the laws of levirate marriage). When Boaz discovered Ruth the next morning he praised her for her loyalty to the family. He did not marry her right away because there was a closer relative who had the right to levirate marriage. The man declined his right to marry Ruth and Boaz proceeded to marry her. For her actions, Ruth is highly praised.[3]

Let us look at the results of Tamar and Ruth's actions. Tamar had two sons with Judah, Peretz and Zerach. Peretz was an

---

1   Genesis 38:6–26.
2   Ruth 1:16–17.
3   Book of Ruth.

ancestor of Boaz. Ruth had a son with Boaz named Oved, who was the father of King David and therefore the ancestor of the Messiah. We read the story of Ruth every year on Shavuot, the holiday which commemorates Israel's acceptance of the Torah.

Tamar and Ruth used their sexual power to correct the world, to shape the world according to Torah values. Their motives were absolutely pure. The result is that they paved the way for Redemption, for it is through their line that the Messiah will come. As Tamar Frankiel describes in her book, *The Voice of Sarah,*

> The stories tell us not merely that women are sensual and can use that power to men's detriment. That would...certainly not....be admired. Rather, they tell us sexuality is holy, to be used only in the service of holiness; and women have direct access to that holy power. From this deep view of women's bodies comes the high Jewish valuation of marriage and sex only within marriage.... The woman who knows her sexuality and her inner, spiritual self can recognize her true purpose in life, can act with power and confidence at any moment, and can thereby affect her own destiny, the destiny of her people, and that of the whole world.[1]

Women's Three Mitzvot

The way the *akeret habayit* sanctifies each aspect of being is symbolized and epitomized by the three mitzvot given particularly to women: separating challah, lighting the Shabbat candles, and observing *taharat hamishpachah*.

---

1   Tamar Frankiel, *The Voice of Sarah: Feminine Spirituality and Traditional Judaism* (New York: Biblio Press, 1990), 35–36.

Challah

When the Temple stood, the *kohanim* and *levi'im*, the priests and the Levites, were to devote themselves exclusively to its service. All the other Jews, the Israelites, were required to support them. One of the ways they were commanded to do this was by separating a piece of dough, called *challah*, every time they made dough with at least 3.5 pounds of flour. In order to partake of this *challah*, the *kohanim* and *levi'im* had to be *tahor*, ritually pure. There are many levels of being *tahor*, and it is now impossible for *kohanim* and *levi'im* to attain the necessary level required in order to eat *challah* because the Temple no longer stands. However, the commandment to separate the *challah* remains. Instead of giving it to the *kohanim* and *levi'im*, we burn it and throw it out so as not to derive any benefit from it.

The commandment of taking *challah* applies equally to men and women. However, since it is usually the woman who makes bread for her family, it is usually she who performs this mitzvah. But that is not why it is considered a woman's mitzvah.

Bread is considered the "staff of life"; it is the symbol of all nourishment. Food is generally a female-controlled resource. It is a medium of nurturing, showing love, and providing security. When a woman separates *challah*, the rest of the dough and by extension the rest of her food becomes a medium of worshiping God. As Tamar Frankiel writes in her book, *The Voice of Sarah*,

> [Separating challah] puts all our nurturing, giving, bonding activities around food in a different perspective.... [I]f we take from our bread, the staff of life, this small portion of *challah*, we are giving a special kind of *tzedakah*, or charity from the heart of life. We give it, symbolically now, to

nourish the work of the Temple because the Temple...represents the center of holiness, the womb of our spiritual life.... [W]e dedicate our bread to the holy work of nourishing our souls as well as our bodies. The rest of the bread will be taken to our table, the extension of the Temple altar and the echo of Sarah's tent, to become the center of holy nourishment in our own families and communities.[1]

Shabbat Candles

There is something very special about Shabbat candles. There they stand, humble yet regal, a connection to our tradition and the beacon light of our future. Candles are always nice. They always add a certain mystery and beauty to the atmosphere. Yet Shabbat candles add something more − some sublime otherworldly serenity we feel in the recesses of our soul.

By lighting Shabbat candles we welcome the Shabbat into our home. Those two little flames illuminate our homes and our souls with the spiritual light of Shabbat − the source of Jewish continuity, unity, and sanity. The traditional time to light is eighteen minutes before sunset − the official starting time of the Shabbat. In this way, one can take a portion of secular time and add it to holy time, like when one takes *challah*.

Every Jew, man and woman, is obligated to light Shabbat candles. When people live together, one person can light for the entire household. If that person has in mind that she is lighting for all the others and they have in mind that they are included in that individual's lighting, then the other people are considered as having fulfilled their obligation.

In a family setting, it is the woman of the house who lights

1 Frankiel, *The Voice of Sarah*, 78.

the candles. This is considered her prerogative, and no one else can light them for her unless she is unable to do so. One explanation of why this mitzvah devolves on the woman is that the woman's lighting these physical candles is symbolic of how she illuminates her home and the lives of her family members with Torah. Also, lighting the Shabbat candles is a private affair, which fits right in with a woman's private role, and the moments right after lighting are considered the most auspicious time for prayer. By lighting the Shabbat candles, the woman inaugurates the Shabbat in her home.

Taharat HaMishpachah

Observing the laws of *taharat hamishpachah* requires brutal honesty and meticulously detailed preparations. A rabbi is available to answer questions and a *mikveh* lady makes sure the immersion is kosher (since it is impossible for the woman herself to tell). Besides that, the observance of these laws relies entirely on the woman's fear of God.

Through the mitzvah of challah, the woman can sanctify the world of objects. By lighting candles, the woman sanctifies time. By observing the laws of *taharat hamishpachah*, she sanctifies action. Then, God rests His presence, the *Shechinah*, in her home and sanctifies the space. In this way, the woman causes all aspects of existence to ascend to holiness.

How a Husband and Wife Create a Mikdash Me'at

A husband and wife must strive to make their home a *mikdash me'at*, a miniature Sanctuary. Here we will take a deeper look at what this means and the unique ways a husband

and wife contribute to this goal. The following description of the Sanctuary and the Temple, as well as the roles of the Temple and the Sanhedrin, are based on Rabbi Aryeh Kaplan's book, *Jerusalem: The Eye of the Universe*.[1]

Both the Jewish home and the Sanctuary/Temple have to be built using the same spiritual "blueprint." Therefore, it is not exactly correct to say that the home should be modeled after the Sanctuary. Rather, both are variations on a theme. The first Jewish home, the tent of Sarah, predated the building of the Temple by two thousand years.

Sarah was a holy person and imbued all her activities with such holiness that she merited miracles to occur in her home constantly, the same miracles that would occur later in the Temple. There was a blessing in her dough — guests who ate of it were satisfied for a long time afterward. This paralleled the loaves of showbread that were placed in the Temple which were eaten a week after being baked and yet retained all their freshness and warmth during the week.

When Sarah lit her Shabbat lamp, it remained lit the entire week. The following Shabbat, she would light it again — thereby adding another layer of holiness. This was paralleled by the western lamp of the Temple menorah — it was the first to be lit and the last to go out. It would then be relit the following day. The cloud of the *Shechinah*, the symbol of God's presence, rested over her tent. This was the same cloud that rested over the Sanctuary.[2]

Also, both Abraham's and Sarah's open doors extended a

1   Aryeh Kaplan, *Jerusalem: The Eye of the Universe* (New York: National Conference of Synagogue Youth/Union of Orthodox Jewish Congregations of America, 1976).
2   Artscroll Tanach Series, *Bereishis*, vol. 3 (New York: Mesorah Publications Ltd., 1978), 837.

welcome to all passersby.[1] This symbolized how the Temple beckoned every Jew to come in and draw closer to God. These miracles were due to her merit, and they stopped when she died. They only resumed when Rebekah, her successor, entered her tent and became its *akeret habayit*, and acted in as holy manner as Sarah.

In describing the seventh day of creation, the Torah says, "And He [God] abstained on the seventh day from all His work [*melachah*] which He had done."[2] From here we learn that *melachah* is defined as God's act of Creation. When the Jews built the Sanctuary while they were in the desert, all the categories of labor that went into its building were also termed *melachah*. In fact, the exact definition of *melachah* in Jewish law is derived from all the types of labor that went into building the Sanctuary. The Sanctuary was a microcosm of all of creation. Building the Sanctuary was meant to parallel God's act of creation and therefore employed every type of *melachah*. This made Man a partner with God in the creation and the completion/perfection of the world.

Likewise, the home is a microcosm of creation. In building a home, the husband and wife recreate the act of Creation. First, the act of marriage takes two halves of a human being and combines them into one complete whole. Then, as they develop their relationship and build their *shalom bayit*, they are literally building their own temple. The *Shechinah*, God's presence which dwelled in the Sanctuary, dwells with them as well. When they have children, they become partners with God

---

1 Abraham and Sarah had separate "tents." These were no ordinary tents, but places of learning. Abraham taught the men about God, while Sarah taught the women. See *Bereishit Rabbah* on Genesis 2:18.

2 Genesis 2:2.

in a reenactment of Creation.

In the Temple there was the *mizbe'ach*, the altar on which animals were sacrificed. When a person sins, her animal nature takes over. To act as if one has no free will is to deny one's humanity and Divine spark. One lowers herself even below the level of an animal, who at least does not sin.

In order to correct a wrong, a person has to first admit her error, then confess it to God, then feel remorse over what she did and promise not to do it again. She has to ask forgiveness from all whom she hurt and make reparations as best as she could. She also has to work on herself so as not to commit the sin again in the future. The final step of the repentance process is to return her animal nature to its Source, meaning that from now on she will use her animal nature in the service of God.[1] When the Temple stood, this was done by taking an animal and returning it to its Source by offering it as a sacrifice.

One effect of sinning is that the resulting guilt causes a person to feel far from God. For example, after Adam and Eve sinned, they felt the need to distance themselves from their Creator by hiding from Him. A sacrifice is called a *korban*, which has the same root as *karov*, near. The effect of the sacrifice was meant to repair the relationship between the person and God so as to help the person to draw near to God.

God specifically commanded that the *mizbe'ach* be made from uncut stones: "And when you make for Me an altar of stones, do not build them hewn, for you will have raised your sword over it and desecrated it."[2] The sword, and by extension

---

1   An example of how one's animal nature can be used in the service of God is the observance of the laws of kashrut to sanctify the very animal activity of eating.

2   Exodus 20:22.

all warfare, is the result of Man's subjugating his intellectual nature to service his animal nature. Since the *mizbe'ach* was meant to rectify a person's animal nature, it had to be made with natural stones. If the sword was introduced to the stones for the *mizbe'ach*, it might have sullied them with Man's barbaric impulses. The sacrifices would not have been able to rectify Man's animal side, and the whole sacrificial system would have become an act of brutality.

The Sages compared the woman to the *mizbe'ach*: "The modest woman atones for her household like the *mizbe'ach*."[1] How does a person give in to sin in the first place? We learn from Adam and Eve that sin is a result of being blinded by one's perception of reality and ignoring God's will. When one follows God's commandments and learns His will as expressed in the Torah, one is able to look beyond the flashing lights of a false reality and get a glimpse of the Truth. Modesty is about looking past what is on the outside and seeing that which is within. This means looking past a person's appearance and seeing her Divine spark. It also means directing one's animal nature, particularly one's sexuality, which is the most unruly aspect of one's animal nature, to the service of God. A woman who is modest and infuses her home with the principles of modesty helps prevent her family from sinning and helps them atone when they have sinned.

Past the *mizbe'ach* was the inner chamber, the Heichal. The Heichal contained the golden menorah, a golden altar for incense, and a special table for the showbread. The showbread was laid out in the beginning of the week and eaten the following Sabbath by the priests. A miracle occurred so that even after a whole week, the bread tasted like it was fresh from the oven. In

1 *Tanchuma, Vayishlach* 6.

the home, the woman's mitzvah of lighting the Sabbath candles parallels the menorah. Her mitzvah of taking challah parallels the showbread.

Past the inner chamber was the Holy of Holies. Inside it were the ark of the covenant, the two tablets with the Ten Commandments, and the original Torah that Moses wrote according to the word of God. The Holy of Holies was also called the "bedroom," meaning that it was the most private area of the sanctuary and it allowed Israel and God to completely unite. The woman's mitzvah of *taharat hamishpachah* sanctifies the intimate relations between her and her husband and allows them to achieve a perfect union, thereby transforming their own bedroom into a "Holy of Holies."

The Ten Commandments and the original Torah scroll are the physical testimony, the witnesses to God's covenant with Israel. The mother is like the written Torah. It is she who must teach her children that the covenant is a physical reality. She inculcates the most profound beliefs about Judaism in her children. From her the children learn about a personal, caring God who has a special relationship with the Jewish people. She is the first to introduce them to mitzvot and the idea that they have a responsibility to act in a holy manner. We will explore how the mother and father contribute to the education of their children in a subsequent chapter.

If the home is like the sanctuary, then the woman is its priestess. Just like the *kohanim* were charged with all the duties concerning the sanctuary so that it could be a place through which God could dwell in Israel, so the *akeret habayit* is responsible for making her home a place where her family can attain holiness. The *kohanim* were commanded by God to bless the people in a special way. While the Torah makes it clear that the blessing comes from God, not from the *kohanim*, giving this blessing allows the *kohanim* to become conduits of blessing. Likewise, the Sages say that the *akeret habayit* is the source of all blessing in a home.[1]

Because the priests' responsibilities were so vital, they were exempt from many commandments which would interrupt their service. For example, they were exempt from army service and earning a livelihood (they were supported from special tithes paid by the people). Likewise, one reason the woman is exempt from many time-bound commandments is because they would interfere with her responsibilities at home.

Built into the outer wall of the Temple, not far from the *mizbe'ach*, was the Chamber of Cut Stone where the Sanhedrin sat, taught, and judged. The Sanhedrin was the central legislative and judicial body of Israel. They could enact religious law. They also acted as a supreme court and were the final authority on all matters of Torah law. Their key role was to preserve, interpret, and teach the oral law. The Torah has a written and an oral part. The Torah is meant to teach a person how to act in accordance with God's will. Like any teaching, one needs both written notes and practical experience. While the written Torah talks about the existence of the covenant, it is the oral law which details how to live by the covenant.

The oral Torah was passed down orally until about two thousand years ago. At that time, the Jews were persecuted so much that it was impossible for the majority of people to devote the necessary time to studying the oral tradition. The Sages feared that it would be lost entirely, and so they made the decision to write it down. After three hundred years, the writing, called the "Mishnah," was completed. Later, commentaries on

1   *Sanhedrin* 22a–b.

the Mishnah were written down as well and that is called "Gemara." The Mishnah and Gemara together are called the "Talmud."

The Chamber of Cut Stone had to be built into the Temple so that half of it was inside the Temple, and half of it was outside of it. From the chamber, one could enter the Temple directly. This was necessary because sometimes questions would come up during services. The *kohanim* could not leave the Temple, and so the Sanhedrin had to be easily accessible and able to enter the Temple immediately. Part of the chamber had to be outside the Temple because the Sanhedrin had to sit when they judged, and one is forbidden from sitting in the Temple. There is also a requirement that the Sanhedrin be near the *mizbe'ach*.

The place where the Sanhedrin operated had to be made specifically of cut stone, as the name of the chamber suggests. The Sanhedrin represented the oral Torah. The oral Torah is the part of the tradition that is always interpreted and applied to new situations by Man. For this reason, God wanted the chamber to be infused with Man's intellect. There was no concern that in doing so Man's base nature would taint the stone because studying the oral Torah is the antidote to the evil inclination. It is the way Man uses his intellect to serve God and not his animal desires. Making the chamber out of stones that were cut by Man began the process of properly channeling his creativity to his Creator.

The man's role at home is like that of the Sanhedrin. It is he who is the primary teacher of exactly how the commandments are to be kept. He is also the decisor of Jewish law at home. This does not mean he can arbitrarily interpret the law any way he wants. However, there are usually a number of legitimate ways to decide and he chooses which opinion his family will follow.

The ideal of the husband and wife team is the *kohen gadol*, the high priest. The *kohen gadol* was also a member of the Sanhedrin. This one person represented both the priesthood and the Sanhedrin. While the husband and wife have distinct roles at home, they are not meant to act like two different institutions. Rather, they have to completely integrate their roles and unite into a whole human being.

Eve: The Woman's Second Name

There are three partners in a child's birth: the father, the mother, and God.[1]

As we mentioned earlier, the Torah tells us that God "built" the woman. The word for "built" is *banah*, which is related to the word *bein*, which means "between." A woman is the link between the generations. It is she who builds the future.

Each infant is granted a perfect soul which strives towards the spiritual, as well as a physical body which inclines toward the material.[2] After the sin in the Garden of Eden, a person has had to work very hard at being good, while being evil has come relatively easily. Everyone therefore needs much guidance from birth as to the proper path to follow. A child needs a lot of attention and guidance in order to develop his or her spiritual potential. Enter the mother.

"The man called his wife Eve (*Chavah*) because she had become the mother of all living."[3] The word *Chavah* is in the present tense, meaning that being a mother is an ongoing job of not

---

1   *Kohelet Rabbah* 5.
2   Rabbi Moshe Chaim Luzzatto, *The Way of God* (Jerusalem: Feldheim Publishers, 1983), 45
3   Genesis 3:20.

only giving birth to an infant, but causing it to live.

On the simplest level, this means that from conception onward, the infant is dependent on the mother for survival. All the mother's efforts to take care of the baby's physical needs go beyond ensuring immediate survival; she has the power to place the child on the path to a lifetime of health. Studies have shown that a mother's diet during pregnancy greatly influences the newborn's health. Also, a mother's milk contains all the nutrients a baby needs and also passes antibodies to the child. In this way, a mother causes her baby to live.

A mother has the power to develop a child's emotional and intellectual life. Studies have shown that a person's lifetime emotional and intellectual potential is set by age three. What determines this potential is the amount and quality of stimulation the baby receives. Due to her deep connection to the baby and her maternal instinct, as well as her proximity at this time, a mother has the most influence on the child.

All of Judaism rests on the belief of a loving God who is intimately concerned with every detail of His creation. It is the mother who inculcates this belief in her child. It is she who instills a love of God and His Torah and a fear of heaven in her child. This is one interpretation of what the Sages were talking about when they said, "A woman's wisdom is in her weaving."[1] Weaving is a process by which separate threads are inextricably combined into a single fabric. Likewise, a mother weaves the threads of Torah into her child, making them an inherent part of his or her being.[2]

The word for life is *chaim*, which is in the plural. The word

---

1   *Yoma* 66b.
2   Sarah Shapiro, *Growing with My Children* (Southfield, MI: Targum Press, Inc., 1990), 325.

for death, *mavet*, is in the singular. This teaches us that one who is truly living in this world will also have a second "life" in the world to come. Death would only be a means of ascending to a higher level of existence. The way to achieve true living is by living a life of Torah. Therefore, by placing her children on the path to Torah, the mother causes them to live in this world and acts as their midwife to "deliver" them to the world to come.

A Mother in Israel

Judaism was started by fathers and mothers. The book of Genesis, which describes the beginnings of the Jewish people, is a story about families. It is in the context of family life that Judaism is forged. Abraham and Sarah, Isaac and Rebekah, Jacob and Rachel and Leah saw parenthood as the quintessential way in which they could shape the Jewish people. They understood that their every act as parents would reverberate throughout the generations. We see this in how Abraham cried out to God after He promised him wealth and worldly fame. He had everything that leaders of other religions had: he was a great thinker — the proponent of monotheism, a charismatic character, respected by the nations as a "prince of God."[1] And yet he cried out to God, "What can You give me, seeing that I go childless?"[2]

It is hard to believe that one's own actions as a parent will have an affect of the same magnitude. However, one can look at one's grandparents and see how their actions affected one's parents, and how in turn one's parents affected one's self. An action could have been as drastic as moving to a different country or as subtle as the tone of voice used in the home. Let us remember

1   Genesis 23:6.
2   Ibid. 15:2.

that one's grandparents had parents who shaped them, and our great-grandparents had parents who shaped them, and so on. One can now see how she is the result of generations and generations of parenting, all the way back to Abraham and Sarah. It may be frightening to contemplate, but one's actions today will likewise affect generations and generations.

Judaism has been around for close to four thousand years. Jews have always been a small, often despised minority. It is a miracle that we still exist. One reason for this is the strong families Jews have had, particularly the commitment of the parents to raise children to be good Jews. No wonder such an emphasis is placed on parenthood.

The Torah goes further to say that a man is obligated to have children.[1] The woman is not obligated for reasons discussed below. Since a human being is created in the image of God, one who does not have children is said to decrease God's image, and it is as if he had shed blood.[2] This is because the world is in a natural state of deterioration, and if a man does not build it then it is as if he worked to destroy it.

Some of the reasons why women are exempt from having children are: 1) It endangers their life and the Torah does not command us to regularly put our lives in danger.[3] 2) In order to have children, the woman may have to pursue the man. Since this goes counter to many women's nature, the Torah does not require it.[4] 3) A woman has a natural desire to have children, so it is not something she needs to be commanded to do.[5]

---

1 Genesis 9:7.

2 *Yevamot* 63b.

3 *Meshech Chochmah* on Genesis 9:1.

4 *Yevamot* 65b.

5 *Kiddushin* 29b.

Certainly there is a very strong cultural pressure for the woman to have children. The benefits and rewards to the woman are very great. Having children is a spiritually eye-opening experience that allows a woman to understand God like nothing else can. Raising children also provides the woman with the best way to work on her negative traits and to enhance her positive traits. It also teaches the mother about her relationship to God, our Father.

Children are a divine trust to the parents. They are our guarantors of Torah. Before God gave Israel the Torah, He asked for a guarantee that Israel would keep it. First Israel offered the ancestors as guarantors. God replied, "Your sureties need sureties. I have found fault with them." Israel then offered the prophets, which too were rejected. Finally, Israel offered her children. "In truth, they are good guarantors," replied God. "For their sake I will give [the Torah] to you."[1]

What about people who aren't able to have children?

To many people, the mere thought that they might not be able to have biological children is horrifying. No matter how involved a person is with her career or other interests, most women and men assume that one day they, too, will have a house full of children. This is a dream that people have since childhood. It is the one that remains while others evaporate. This is especially true for Jews since Judaism (not to mention one's parents) puts such a great emphasis on having children. As couples try, and try, and try, and the months of trying become a year, the thought that was never in their minds becomes a fear in the back of their minds, then a fear that is staring them

---

1   *Shir HaShirim Rabbah* 1:4.

in the face, and then a reality that they must deal with.

Judaism has a rich tradition which couples can draw on to deal with infertility. Many people feel that they are the only ones with this problem – it seems that the entire Jewish community is teeming with (everybody else's) children. The first thing a couple can learn from even a cursory knowledge of Jewish sources is that they are not alone. Almost all of the matriarchs – Sarah, Rebekah, and Rachel – suffered from infertility.[1] The Torah documents the resulting agonizing pain of our foremothers and the variety of ways in which they dealt with it. Hannah, the mother of the prophet Samuel, was infertile for many years.[2] Her fervent prayer for a son became the model that the Sages adopted for the central prayer in every service, called the *Amidah*. Today, infertility continues to be a problem for a large segment of the Jewish population.

Obviously, a couple is not considered as having committed a transgression if they don't have children. The commandment only refers to trying to have children. Whether one is successful or not is up to God, and one is certainly not held accountable for something beyond one's control. Many couples struggling with infertility pursue medical treatment, and some adopt. In some communities there are organizations which help infertile couples by providing support groups and/or facilitating adoption. There is also a book entitled *Be Fruitful and Multiply* edited by Dr. Richard M. Grazi[3] of essays by well-known infertility specialists and halachic authorities on the latest medical techniques in

---

1 The fourth matriarch, Leah, was destined to suffer in the same way. However, since she was less loved by Jacob than Rachel, God compensated her for her pain by making her the mother of half the tribes of Israel.

2 I Samuel 1.

3 Richard M. Grazi, M.D., ed., *Be Fruitful and Multiply* (Jerusalem: Feldheim Publishers, 1994).

the field of infertility and their effects on the Torah-observant couple.

A good resource is a rabbi who understands the spiritual and emotional challenges that infertile couples face, the medical options available, and the halachic issues involved. How do you find such a rabbi? If the local rabbi is not capable of handling these issues himself, he might know of someone who is. Also, one can ask other couples who have faced these difficulties to find out whom they turned to.

As important as having biological children is in Judaism, the true offspring of a person are his good deeds[1] and the Torah that he passed on to others. The reason for this is that there are really two worlds — this world and the world to come. Just as a person can bring someone into this world, he can also bring a person into the world to come by teaching him Torah. The teacher is therefore considered a parent as well, and he takes precedence over the biological parents in many respects.[2] As it says in the Talmud, "If [a man's] own lost article and his father's lost article [need attention], his own takes precedence. His own and his teacher's — his own takes precedence; his father's and his teacher's — his teacher's takes precedence, because his father brought him into this world, whereas his teacher, who instructed him in wisdom, brings him to the world to come."[3]

A recent example of a childless woman who became "a mother to thousands" is Sarah Schenirer. She organized the first Jewish school system for girls which gained wide acceptance in the Orthodox world. Because of her, subsequent generations of

1 *Rashi* on Genesis 6:9.
2 This is assuming that one's primary Torah teacher is not the parent. If the parent is the child's primary Torah teacher then she takes precedence over another teacher.
3 *Bava Metzia* 33a.

girls are receiving a formal Torah education for the first time in Jewish history.[1]

The mother and father must raise their children with both love and discipline. Love is required for effective discipline, and discipline is an integral part of love. The mother cannot decide that she will provide the "love" and assign her husband the role of "disciplinarian." First of all, the mother's "love" would only be self-love because the lack of discipline is only meant to spare the mother negative feelings. The father's discipline would also be ineffective since it is not based on a loving relationship with the child. Also, this arrangement causes a distance between father and child, and it causes the child to not have the proper awe of his mother.

The Torah states that one should "fear his mother and his father"[2] and to "respect his father and his mother."[3] There is a tendency to fear one's father more than one's mother and to respect one's mother more than one's father. Since one must fear and respect both parents equally, the Torah reverses the order. It is the parents' responsibility to teach these commandments to their children, and they can only do this if they both provide love and discipline.

---

1 There have been numerous women who were scholars throughout the ages. Also, all women were taught the basics they needed to live a Jewish life. However, the level of education beyond the basics of the general population of women has been very sensitive to cultural and economic conditions. Most, but not all, cultures where Jews have lived frowned on education for women, and most Jews have usually been very poor. Therefore, the overall level of education has been low for most women at most times and in most places. An excellent book on women's education is *And All Your Children Shall Be Learned: Women and the Study of Torah in Jewish Law and History* by Shoshana Pantel Zolty (Northvale, NJ: Jason Aronson, Inc., 1997).

2 Leviticus 19:13.

3 Exodus 20:12.

Both the father and mother must raise the child to be a good Jew. The mother and father accomplish this in different ways. The Sages tell us to "Listen to the tradition of your father and do not forsake the Torah of your mother."[1] Rabbi Joseph Soloveitchik said in his eulogy of a *rebbetzin*:

> People are mistaken in thinking that there is only one *Massorah* [tradition] and one *Massorah* community; the community of the fathers. It is not true. We have two *Massorot* [pl. of *Massorah*], two traditions, two communities, two *shalshalot hakabbalah* [chains of receiving the tradition] — the *massorah* community of the fathers and that of the mothers.[2]

The mother teaches the experience of the revelation at Sinai. This is a prerequisite to observing the Torah with the proper awe of God. The mother passes on her tradition, her "Torah of the mothers," more by example through the atmosphere that she creates in her home. As Rabbi Soloveitchik continues in his eulogy,

> I used to watch [my mother] arranging the house in honor of a holiday. I used to see her recite prayers; I used to watch her recite the *sidra* every Friday night and I still remember the nostalgic tune. I learned from her very much.... Most of all I learned [from my mother] that Judaism expresses itself not only in formal compliance with the law but also in a living experience. She taught me that there is a flavor, a scent and warmth to mitzvot. I learned from her the most important thing in life — to feel the presence of the

---

1 Proverbs 1:8.
2 Joseph Soloveitchik, "A Tribute to the Rebbitzen of Telne," *Tradition* 17, no. 2 (Spring 1978), 76.

Almighty, and the gentle pressure of His hand resting upon my frail shoulders.[1]

The father teaches the content of the revelation at Sinai — how the Jew must fulfill his/her covenant with God. He passes on the teachings of the Torah and Talmud — he teaches how to read the text, he explains the underlying structure and logic of the laws, and he provides the intellectual discipline required to analyze and apply the law. In other words, the father provides the child the formal instruction in how to live a Jewish life. For example, he would teach his child about the Shabbat by studying its laws with him or her in a methodical manner. This is the "tradition of the fathers."

The importance of the father's teaching is obvious, while the importance of the mother's teaching may seem vague. However, the Torah itself emphasizes in very strong terms the importance of remembering for all generations not only the laws that God taught, but the way in which the Jews experienced the giving of these laws.[2]

> Only beware for yourself and greatly beware for your soul, lest you forget the things that your eyes have beheld and lest you remove them from your heart all the days of your life; and make them known to your children and your children's children — the day that you stood before Hashem, your God, at Horeb, when Hashem said to me, "Gather the people to Me and I shall let them hear My words, so that they shall learn to fear Me all the days that they live on the

---

1 Ibid.

2 The Jews heard the first two of the Ten Commandments directly from God. They found this to be so overwhelming that they asked Moses to learn the Torah directly from God and then teach it to them (Deuteronomy 5:22–24).

earth, and they shall teach their children."[1]

God could have simply said that we must be careful to remember His words and to transmit them to our children. However, He stresses that we must pass down the actual experience of standing in God's presence and receiving His revelation.

The success of the father's teaching depends on the success of the mother's. For this reason, God commanded Moses to teach the Torah to the women first.[2] The mother lays the foundation, and if it is not strong then whatever building the father builds on top of that will be weak. For example, if a child does not have a clear concept of what the Shabbat means and a deep appreciation for its beauty, then learning about the laws of Shabbat would be a dry, meaningless, intellectually numbing mental exercise instead of the rich tradition that it is.

Certainly the father teaches by example, and the mother can give formal instruction. The goal is to teach a child "according to his way,"[3] that is, in whatever way that works. The Torah does not exclude either parent from using a particular method of instruction; it only states how the mother and father generally influence the child the most.

Personal Reflections

Soon after I became religious, I read Betty Friedan's *The Feminine Mystique*. Here was a book about what happened to American women in 1950s suburbia who believed that being a homemaker was the greatest thing they could do. It described

---

1   Deuteronomy 4:9–10.
2   Exodus 19:3.
3   Proverbs 22:6.

the emptiness, the vast emptiness of their lives. And here I was, having just accepted upon myself a religion that preaches the same thing. *Dear God*, I thought, *what have I gotten myself into?* My first impulse was to think, *Well, I got into it, I could get out.* That, I realized, was not an option. Just who would I be kidding? The fact was, I really believed that I was obligated in all the commandments. Would I now stop keeping Shabbat? Would I no longer keep kosher? Would I go back to wearing miniskirts? No. I was stuck.

But then, it occurred to me that the housewife that Betty Friedan was describing was entirely different from the Jewish *akeret habayit*. The goal of these housewives was to have a spotless home, gourmet meals, all the right after-school lessons for their kids, and blond hair. They were not allowed any outside interests. They were not allowed to have their own opinions. Being a maid/cook/chauffeur was supposed to fulfill them. Their relationships with their husbands were just as shallow. No wonder they felt empty!

An *akeret habayit* is an educator, a role model, a negotiator, the very glue that keeps a family together. It is she who infuses her home with Torah. Yes, she cooks and cleans and chauffeurs, but those are only some of the ways in which she builds *shalom bayit*. They are a means to an end, not the end in itself. Her main job is more of a spiritual, intellectual, and emotional nature.

Women are also encouraged to develop outside interests and they certainly are expected to have their own opinions. Since Judaism has a sophisticated understanding of men and women, this knowledge allows husbands and wives to understand, appreciate, and bond with each other in a way they otherwise could not. The laws of *taharat hamishpachah* are just one example of this. So really, I had nothing to worry about. Betty Friedan's book did not apply to me. I have been married for two and a half years now and I have never felt as alive, as fulfilled as I do now.

Still, it did take me a long time to appreciate the woman's role as an *akeret habayit*. How can women be respected in Judaism when their primary role is seen as being "just a housewife"? Maybe Judaism was giving nice lip service about how important a housewife was, including calling her a more impressive sounding "*akeret habayit*," but I didn't really buy it. The bias against housewives was very much ingrained in me. Women should strive to be doctors, lawyers, CEO's, even truck drivers — anything but housewives.

What changed my impression was my experience. I went to the homes of many religious people for Shabbos, and I observed how these women carried themselves and how their husbands treated them. These women were strong and carried themselves with an enormous amount of self-respect. Their husbands treated them with love and respect as equals and not as their servants. This didn't seem to be in spite of what the Torah taught but because of it.

Also, even though the husbands were obviously considered the heads of the families, they did not consider it beneath themselves to clear the table or wash the floor, for instance. In other traditional societies, men would never do "women's work" because it would be beneath them. Here, even though the women would do most of the housework, men would help out as needed. The stigma of "women's work" just wasn't there, rather household chores were considered an important part of life. Even though I couldn't yet understand it intellectually, I saw that Judaism really did appreciate the importance of the woman's role as an *akeret habayit.*

When I first got married and became an *akeret habayit* myself, I often imagined a prereligious alter-ego me observing me and asking me questions loaded with feminist suspicion. Why is my husband sitting at the head of the table? Why is it he who gives a *d'var Torah* (short lecture on the weekly Torah portion)? Why do you sit at the side and serve him food? This alter ego would taunt me, and I had to answer her over and over again.

My husband sits at the head of the table because he is the head of the household. No, this doesn't mean that he gets to be the dictator of our home. It means that he is the representative of our home to the outside world. He gives the *d'var Torah* because he is obligated to study Torah constantly and I am not. Yes, I can give a *d'var Torah* and he encourages me to, but I am not going to take it on as a commandment because I am plenty busy fulfilling the commandments I am obligated in already.

Once, after my husband finished giving his *d'var Torah*, our guest turned to me and asked slightly mockingly, "And where is your *d'var Torah*?"

I waved my hand over the table with the challahs which took me five hours to bake and which I had to schedule my Sunday afternoon around, the food I stayed up till midnight to prepare, and the lovely table setting made possible by generous bridal shower gifts. "This is my *d'var Torah*," I answered.

Serving food always seemed like such a servile thing to do. When I would see other women do it, I felt a combination of pity for them and rage at the situation. But when I do it, I don't feel servile at all. I worked hard to cook that food and I feel like an artist proudly presenting her masterpiece before an appreciative audience. It is also an expression of love, of nurturing, and what's so terrible about that? The same holds true for all the other housework I do. I feel like a farmer working her land. That means getting my hands dirty and doing some things which I don't find particularly pleasant, but at the end of the day I'm proud of the home I made with my own hands.

Over time, my scoffing alter ego faded away. This concerned me at first. Have I accepted the status quo so much that I was getting lazy about challenging myself and searching for answers? No, I realized that wasn't it. I had a wonderful husband who loved and respected me and whom I loved and respected. This relationship was the way it was due to the Torah, not in spite of it. I realized that I was finally able to completely internalize what I had been telling myself.

People often ask me, "What was it that made you become religious?" Well, here is one important piece to the answer.

In college, I took a course in cultural anthropology. Combined with what I knew about other cultures, it showed me that societies were constructed in such a way that only the man's needs were considered, while the woman was treated as an object for his use. For example, in China, women's feet were bound until the women could no longer walk because men found small feet attractive. In parts of Africa, women were castrated so they would not feel sexual pleasure and therefore not be tempted to cheat on their husbands. This practice has received international attention only recently. In Christianity and Islam, men have the right to their wives' bodies and the women must "do their duty" to the men.

What really struck me about Jewish law was that it was the husband's responsibility to sexually satisfy his wife. The wife

174

had no such obligations to her husband. And the rabbis went into details about how to go about doing this: first with words, then with foreplay, and so on. There is a story of a woman who gave birth to very righteous children. When she was asked how she was able to do it, she answered that it was because her husband paid exceptional attention to give her pleasure even at the expense of his own. When I heard this I thought, *A man could not possibly have written this law!* Men as a group aren't known for their understanding of women's needs. And even if they did understand, they certainly would not legislate that women's needs be put ahead of their own, especially when it came to sex.

At first glance, this law may seem to produce an imbalance in the relationship against the man. In a truly equal relationship, shouldn't both the husband and wife have responsibilities to please each other? But nature is not equal. Naturally speaking, men are pretty much guaranteed that their needs will be met. Nothing will happen if they are not ready and if they are not interested. Women have no guarantees. They can be forced to have sex and their pleasure can be entirely absent from the act. With this law, the inequality in nature is corrected and both the husband and wife are satisfied.

It is one thing to philosophize about how women are human beings equal in value to men. It is quite another to actualize this principle in an area where men have the strongest desire and the least self-control. This was the first time I felt such a clear understanding that the origin of Jewish law was from God.

When I heard that Judaism requires the husband and wife to separate while she is menstruating and for seven days afterwards, it struck me as pure genius. This was before I went to Israel or had any concept of what *taharah, tumah,* or *niddah* meant. What a great way to combat boredom, as well as give both partners some personal space!

As I learned more about all these concepts as well as the Jewish concept of God, why He created the world, and what we were supposed to be doing exactly, I saw a remarkable unity. It all made sense, it all fit together.

Mathematics has recently discovered objects called fractals. If you know what they are, great; if not, look them up – they are beautiful. One of the properties of fractals is something called self-similarity. If you look at a tiny piece of the fractal, any tiny piece, it will look like the whole. An example in nature is a tree. If you look at a branch or a subbranch, it will look like the whole tree. The more I learned about Judaism's view of the world, the more I saw this self-similarity in everything – both the spiritual and physical worlds.

A lot of the things I had learned finally clicked when I first went to the *mikveh*. Finally, I was doing something that I studied so much about which was supposed to have such an immense impact on me, my family, and the Jewish people. It was one of the three mitzvot which characterized my unique contribution. I'm not even going to try to explain how I felt. There was such a sense of awe, it was beyond words.

But that's when I really understood that I had nothing to be jealous of from the mitzvot that men do. They may worship God by wrapping a tefillin around their arm and head, they may put the tallit over their shoulders, they may wear the yarmulke on their head. But I was worshiping God with my entire body.

But more than that, I felt like I touched something both beyond myself and deep within myself. I had touched the Divine.

Chapter 5

Prayer

Initial Stumbling Blocks

One of the first encounters women have with traditional Judaism, and one of the most distasteful, occurs in the synagogue. First, there's that terrible *mechitzah*. Often, the *mechitzah* not only separates the sexes but obstructs the woman's vision of what is going on and makes it difficult to hear the prayer leader. Sometimes it seems that women are in a different room altogether. Then there's the fact that only men are allowed to lead services and read from the Torah. A woman isn't even counted in a minyan, the group of ten men necessary to worship in a public manner. A woman might feel like a second-class citizen and a spectator where she believes she should be an active participant.

The Synagogue's Place in Jewish Life

We are so immersed in American society that we think its understanding of religion, based on Christianity, is applicable to Judaism. The Church is the center of Christian life: it is the molder of its philosophy, it is the center of its worship, it is termed the House of God. Attendance at Sunday services is the indicator of how religious a Christian is. When looking at Judaism, one may assume that the synagogue is the Jewish version of the church. This is completely wrong.

The center of Jewish life is the Torah. The Torah has commandments concerning every detail of life, from when one arises in the morning to when one goes to sleep at night. It includes ritual laws such as the laws of Shabbat and ethical laws such as how to treat other people. Religiosity is measured by how well one fulfills all these commandments. A House of God is any place where one acts in a holy manner. This can be a place of business, a home, or a synagogue. The main institution where the Torah is taught and practiced and passed on to the next generation is the home. In fact, both the home and the synagogue are modeled after the Temple.

In Judaism, there are standard morning, afternoon, and evening services, which consist of a number of prayers. Each service has a "public" version and a "private" version. The public version is just like the private version, but with the addition of certain prayers which are meant to publicly sanctify God's name. For now, the term *prayer* will refer exclusively to the public version of the standard prayer service. The reason for this is that the restrictions we will be examining only apply to this type of prayer.

One of the Jewish man's obligations is to pray with a minyan. (Once again, the prayer referred to here is a standard service. Personal prayers can be said at any time.) The role of the synagogue is to be a place where this commandment can be fulfilled. Going to the synagogue is not a commandment in itself.

Therefore, men would not go to a synagogue for a service unless they were fairly certain that there would be a minyan (there might not always be a minyan, which may happen in a small community).

The synagogue is an important arena where men fulfill their role of sanctifying God in a public manner. However, the home is the major arena where women fulfill their role of sanctifying God in a private manner. Therefore, it is misleading to view the roles of men and women in synagogue life as representative of their position in Jewish life or society.

Mechitzah

A *mechitzah* is a separation in the synagogue between the men and women. It can be some type of partition that comes up at least till the shoulder, or it can be a balcony where the women would sit. The function of the *mechitzah* is to prevent improper behavior between the sexes (i.e., gazing, flirting, and anything else that would take one's mind off of praying to God) in the synagogue. Since it is usually the men who gaze at women and initiate the improper behavior, the rabbis were much more concerned about the men not being able to see the women than vice versa.

One might argue that just sitting next to someone is not arousing. However, just remembering how you felt when you sat in class next to the boy you had a crush on is enough to see that this isn't true.

One might also argue that "the family that prays together stays together." This is not a Jewish concept. The centrality of the family to Judaism has been demonstrated. The way a family stays together is by working as a team to do mitzvot — helping the poor, welcoming guests, celebrating the holidays. Ultimately, however, each member of the family must develop a personal relationship with God through prayer.

One might also play devil's advocate and say that if improper behavior is not to be tolerated, then the *mechitzah* should not allow women to see the men either. It may seem that the Rabbis were not sufficiently sensitive to women's feelings in that they were not concerned about them being distracted by the men. The Rabbis understood the different sexual natures of men and women. They realized that while men are very sensitive to a woman's external attractiveness, women are more sensitive to a man's emotional attractiveness. Advertisers know this well. If they want women to feel attracted to a man, they will concentrate on his face, and particularly his eyes — the window to his soul. If they want a man to be attracted to a woman, they will show her entire body as revealed as possible. For this reason, the Rabbis understood that it was the men who were in danger of being distracted by seeing the women and not vice versa.

The requirement of a *mechitzah* does not mean that women should be made to feel uncomfortable in a synagogue. There is no reason why a *mechitzah* should make it difficult to see or hear what is going on or make a woman feel like she is on the "outskirts" of the synagogue. Maybe this was not something that bothered women in the past. However, this issue bothers women, including Orthodox women, a lot, and more modern synagogue designs are sensitive to this. For example, there are several synagogues where the partition is placed in the middle of the synagogue and is made of one-way glass. In this way, the women can see the men and everything that is happening, but the men can't see the women.

However, since synagogues have limited space and money,

they are designed in a utilitarian manner in order to accommodate most of the worshipers most of the time. Most of the worshipers are usually men and they are the ones who come most of the time. Therefore, most of the space is allotted to them. If women want to change the amount of space allotted to the women's section, it would not be enough to only make the demands. They would have to demonstrate that they would actually use that space.

Minyan

The origin of the minyan is the incident of the spies. When the Jews were in the desert, they were about to go into Israel, conquer the people living there, and settle the land. However, they felt insecure in their ability to do this and requested Moses to send out spies. Moses sent twelve men to spy out the land. Of the twelve, ten came back with a negative report and convinced the men that they would not be able to conquer it.[1] The women, however, never believed this report but remained strong in their faith in God. Moses and his court of law learned from this that when Jewish men come together as a group, they can easily act in an evil manner. In order to rectify this, it was decreed that they must come together as a group of at least ten in order to worship God.

The women did not believe the spies. Each woman decided not to join the mob clamoring to go back to Egypt. Therefore, they were not included in the decree. Each woman retained the status of the patriarchs and matriarchs, who prayed to God as individuals. For a woman to insist that she be counted as part of the minyan is ludicrous because it would be like insisting that

---

1 Numbers 13:1–33.

she be held responsible for rectifying an error which her foremothers never committed.[1]

Women's Obligations in Prayer

Another reason why women cannot be included in a minyan is due to their lesser degree of obligation in prayer.

The obligation for men and women to pray every day comes from the Torah. However, the prayer services were instituted over a thousand years after the Torah was given. This was done by the national Jewish court of the time, the Sanhedrin, after the Temple was destroyed. The prayer services were meant to parallel and substitute for the sacrifices which could no longer be offered.

All services start with prayers that praise God. The central prayer in each service is called the *Amidah*. It is composed of nineteen blessings which praise God, make requests on behalf of the individual and the entire nation of Israel, and thank Him for all His blessings. During the morning and evening services a prayer called the "Shema" is said. In this prayer, one proclaims one's love of God and accepts the yoke of God's commandments. The heart of this prayer is the proclamation "Hear, O Israel, the Lord is our God, the Lord is One."[2] Saying the Shema in the morning and evening is an obligation for men which comes from the Torah, not the Sanhedrin.

Men are obligated to pray the entire morning, afternoon, and evening services. The evening services were originally optional, but the men have universally taken on this commandment. When an optional practice is universally done, it acquires

1 Lisa Aiken, *To Be a Jewish Woman* (Northvale, NJ: Jason Aronson, Inc., 1992), 98.
2 Deuteronomy 6:4.

the status of something one is obligated to do.

According to most authorities, women are obligated to say the morning and afternoon *Amidah*.[1] Women are certainly encouraged to say more of the prayer service, if they have the time and inclination. Since evening prayers are not a practice that women have taken upon themselves, it remains truly optional for them.

One reason that women are not required to say the entire prayer service is that they are not obligated to say the Shema. Since the Shema must be said at specific times, it is considered a positive, time-bound mitzvah. In general, women are exempt from positive, time-bound commandments.

Of the 613 commandments that were given, there are seven which fall under this category: saying the Shema prayer, wearing tefillin (phylacteries), wearing fringes on a four-cornered garment (tzitzit), counting the Omer (the days between Passover and Shavuot), hearing the blowing of the shofar on Rosh HaShanah, sitting in the sukkah during the holiday of Sukkot (Tabernacles), and taking a *lulav* (a palm branch with willow and myrtle) and *etrog* (citron) on the first day of Sukkot. Women are encouraged to perform all these commandments with the exception of tzitzit and tefillin.

Several reasons are given as possible explanations for the exemptions. One is that fulfilling these commandments could be very difficult for a woman who manages a household, especially when she has little children.[2] There is a general principal in the Torah that one who is engaged in performing one mitzvah is exempt from performing another mitzvah at that time. Since

---

1   *Mishnah Berurah* 106:4.
2   Abudraham, *Seder Tefilloth Shel Chol*; *Kol Bo*, no. 73; *Sefer Chassidim*, no. 611.

children's demands must be met at all times during the day and night, a woman often cannot control how she uses her time. Obligating her to perform the above-mentioned commandments would require her to be in two places (in the physical or spiritual sense) at the same time. In order to avoid conflict, the Torah makes it clear what takes priority.

Another reason is that the above commandments teach the person about the sanctity and preciousness of time.[1] Women can understand these concepts by virtue of their menstrual cycles — for a short period each month their bodies get ready to create life and in many months this opportunity is lost. A third reason is that men need to constantly occupy themselves with Torah study and mitzvot because of their greater tendencies toward aggression[2] (95 percent plus of the jail population is male).

A fourth reason is given by Rabbi Hirsch, who lived in nineteenth century Germany, and on the surface may seem outdated.[3] He said that men need constant reminders about what their true goal in life is because of their increased contact with society at large and their pursuit of a livelihood. Since women generally stay home, they do not get as much exposure to the non-Jewish world and therefore do not need these reminders to develop their spiritual sensitivity. This may not seem applicable today since women work outside the home as much as men do. Also, with television, magazines, and the Internet, it is very easy to bring the outside world home.

However, this argument still makes sense if we look at it on

---

1 Norman Lamm, *A Hedge of Roses* (Jerusalem: Feldheim Publishers, 1977), 76–78.

2 Maharal, *Drush Al HaTorah.*

3 Rabbi Samson Raphael Hirsch, commentary on Leviticus 23:43.

a deeper level. A man's "pursuit of livelihood" ultimately refers to his public role in Judaism, and a woman's domestic responsibility refers to her private role in Judaism. Due to the public nature of men's role, they may easily slip into the non-Jewish way of thinking and assume that their visibility is a measure of their success. They may think that they are doing their job as long as they look pious to others. By fulfilling these time-bound commandments, they are reminded every day of just who is in charge and who it is they must impress.

Since women have a private role, most people do not see what they do. It is much more difficult for a woman to use other people's opinions to measure her worth. She is much more aware than a man that the measure of her value is how well she fulfills God's will, and not how impressed others are with her. The emphasis for women on *tzeniut* strengthens this understanding.

There is a concept in Judaism that one can fulfill a mitzvah for another only if one has at least the same degree of obligation. For example, both men and women are equally obligated concerning the laws of Shabbat. One of the things one must do in honor of Shabbat is light the Shabbat candles. Since women have the same obligation to observe Shabbat as men, they can light candles on their behalf.

By definition, a minyan must consist of adult men who have the same degree of obligation in prayer. Since a woman's obligation in prayer is less than that of a man, she cannot be counted in a minyan. There are times when a man may not be counted in a minyan. When a man's immediate relative died and has not yet been buried, he is called an *onen*. At this time, he has a lessened obligation in prayer. As such, he may not be counted in a minyan.

Women are considered a "public" when there is a public defamation of God's name because they have an equal obligation in refraining from defaming God's name. For example, if a person would put a gun to a Jew's head and order him to eat pork, the Jew would be allowed to eat the pork. He could violate all but three commandments (forbidding murder, adultery, and idolatry) if there was a threat to life. However, if he was in front of a public, then he would be forbidden from eating the pork because it might cause many others to transgress. Both men and women are counted in this minimum group of ten because they have an equal obligation in refraining from defaming God's name.

Women may also form a public for the public reading of *Megillat Esther* on Purim.[1] *Megillat Esther* tells the story of how the Jews were saved from complete annihilation when they were exiled in Persia. On Purim, it is a mitzvah to publicize this miracle, which is done by reading *Megillat Esther* in public. Women are obligated in this and may therefore come together and read it publicly. However, this should only be done when the women have no other way of hearing it, as it is preferable to hear it with the men.[2]

Why Can't a Woman Be a Prayer Leader?

The reason we need both public and private prayer services

---

1 Rabbi Yitzchak Yaacov Fuchs, *Halichos Bas Yisrael: A Woman's Guide to Jewish Observance,* vol. II (Southfield, MI: Targum Press, Inc., 1987), 194–197.

2 For a complete discussion on this topic, see Alfred Cohen, "Women and the Reading of the Megilla," *Journal of Halacha and Contemporary Society* 30, 25–41.

is because we have to serve God as individuals and as a community. We must sanctify God's name both in the private and the public domain. In order to pray to God in a public manner, one needs a "public." Ten is considered the minimum number of people to constitute a "public." These ten people are viewed as a microcosm of the Jewish nation at large. Since women are just as much a part of the Jewish nation as are men, ten women can be considered a "public." However, since only men are required to sanctify God in the public sphere, only they can be counted towards that "public" in regard to prayer.

The role of the prayer leader is not to pray on behalf of the congregation. He is not seen as closer to God than the other worshipers. His role is to pace the prayers so that everyone is praying the same things at about the same time. He also recites with the congregation the specific prayers that are said only in a minyan.

Unfortunately, in this area the structure of a church has been erroneously applied to a synagogue. In a church, it is often the priest or minister who leads the congregants in prayer. In Judaism, the prayer services are standard and anyone may lead them. Usually the men take turns leading services. A rabbi is treated like any other congregant (although the rabbi of a particular synagogue often has a special seat of honor there). The root of the difference between the two religions is that in Judaism, each individual is seen as having an equal potential to be close to God. There is no "man of God" separate from the others; rather, everyone must strive to live up to his and her potential as beings created in God's image.

There are numerous problems with a woman being a prayer leader. One is that a prayer leader must be part of the minyan. Another problem is the prohibition for men to hear a woman singing.[1] This prohibition is termed *kol ishah*. Since leading services involves singing, this prohibition would also be violated. A third problem is the issue of *tzeniut*. Men may get distracted in their prayer when there is a woman in front of them leading the services. Furthermore, the woman was given the job of developing her inner beauty and this would undermine that mission.

Why Can't a Woman Have an Aliyah?

The Torah is divided into weekly sections, each of which is divided into seven parts called *"aliyot"* (*aliyah* in the singular). When one is assigned for reading a particular part of the weekly portion, one is said to "have an *aliyah*." Three times a week, the Torah is read as part of the morning prayer services.

Originally, the person assigned to this task, the *baal korei*, would recite blessings and "sing" a section of the Torah in front of the congregation. The "notes" that correspond to the text are part of the oral tradition and appear as lines and dots around the Hebrew letters of the text. The Torah is like a very long opera. Over time, the system developed that the person who got the *aliyah* would usually recite just the blessings, while another person would actually read from the Torah.

The main reason women are not allowed to have an *aliyah* is "*kavod tzibbur*,"[2] which roughly means, "the honor of the congregation." Exactly what "*kavod tzibbur*" means is not entirely clear, but there are two possible ways of understanding it. The following is based on *Jewish Woman in Jewish Law* by Moshe Meiselman.[3]

---

1   *Shulchan Aruch, Even HaEzer* 21:1, based on *Berachot* 24a.
2   *Megillah* 23a.
3   Moshe Meiselman, *Jewish Woman in Jewish Law* (New York: Ktav Publishing House, Inc., 1978), 141–144.

When a person prays, she must remove all distractions so that she can concentrate on her words to God. For example, one may not pray the *Amidah*, the central prayer, while holding a baby. Men are forbidden from praying in the presence of immodestly dressed women. When praying, one must also avoid anything which would make her feel self-conscious, for example standing in front of a mirror. The Sages recognized the different ways in which men and women get attracted to each other. While a woman's appearance is a bigger factor for men, a man's personality is the dominant factor for women. Also, people are more self-conscious when they are in the presence of others of the opposite sex than when they are among people of their own sex. In this context, *kavod tzibbur* means being understanding of men's sensitivities and not undermining their prayer.

One may argue that by not giving women an *aliyah* the Sages took away from them an opportunity for prayer and/or religious self-expression. This shows a lack of understanding of their sensitivities, and it undermines their prayer. However, in this context, the concern is not that women will take away opportunities from men. The concern is the distracting effect that their presence in the center of the synagogue will have on the men's ability to concentrate on their prayers. Since a woman will not generally be distracted just by looking at a man, having only men take *aliyot* will not undermine her ability to concentrate on her prayers.

Another interpretation of *kavod tzibbur* is a result of women's lessened obligations in studying Torah. A woman is not obligated to study Torah in the same way that a man is.[1] There are two reasons for studying Torah: to learn how to live as a Jew, and for its own sake. The former reason includes learning

1   *Beit HaLevi*, vol. 1, no. 6.

how to perform mitzvot, proper character traits one must have, as well as more general areas which help one understand one's role as a Jew. Studying is then a means to an end. Women and men are equally obligated in this form of studying.

When studying Torah for its own sake, the studying itself is the goal. This is something which is only obligatory on the men. Included in this commandment is the requirement to constantly toil in Torah study. This is considered the primary purpose in a man's life.

Women are exempt from this form of studying. One reason is their responsibilities in the home. Remember that it is the children who are the guarantors of Torah. If they are not properly raised and educated in living a Torah life, then Torah learning will cease altogether. Raising children is a full-time job (and then some). Also, the woman creates an environment in her home which is conducive to Torah study. Therefore, the woman's responsibilities in her home do not hold her back from Torah. On the contrary, they become a means for her to connect to it. Requiring women to have another full-time job in learning Torah would undermine their roles as mothers and wives and devalue their contribution to Torah scholarship.

In this context, the only people who are allowed to have *aliyot* are those who are maximally obligated in studying Torah — adult Jewish males. To give an *aliyah* to someone who is not maximally obligated would be an infraction of *kavod tzibbur*.

Now the above questions become more relevant: Do the above reasons really justify taking away an opportunity for woman's spiritual growth? In this context, the concern is that women will take opportunities away from men. Recently, Orthodox feminists have addressed this and other concerns surrounding women's limitations in public prayer by organizing women's prayer groups. We will examine these prayer groups in the next section.

There are two other reasons why a woman cannot have an *aliyah*. When the person getting the *aliyah* had to actually sing the Torah portion, there would have been a violation of the law that prohibits a man from hearing a woman sing. Another reason is that the act of getting in front of the congregation and saying the blessings is a very public act which undermines the woman's goals of achieving *tzeniut*.

All these restrictions may seem like an obstacle to a woman's praying because she feels like a spectator to someone else's performance. A woman must ask herself: What is the performance? And who is the performer? A woman must realize that it is she who is the performer, and it is the quality of her prayers which is the performance. It is God who is the spectator and He can be found equally on both sides of the *mechitzah*. He is not impressed with the public show. The only thing that matters to Him is the sincerity of the one praying. The only way this mind-set can be achieved is to learn. Learn. Learn. And learn some more.

Women's Prayer Groups

In the past twenty years, women's prayer groups have become increasingly popular. A lot of the prohibitions concerning women's participation in the synagogue are due to the presence of men. Women's prayer groups allow women to participate in services more fully due to the absence of men. Here we will look at only those groups which abide by the letter of Jewish law.

Since women do not constitute a minyan, the additional

prayers in the public service are not recited. However, being in a prayer group does allow women to lead the services. Also, women can publicly read from the Torah the way men do in a minyan but without the blessings. There is nothing wrong with the Torah being "sung" in front of others, regardless of whether there is a minyan. But it is the blessings which transform it into something which is only permissible in the presence of a minyan.

Women's prayer groups provide women the opportunity to participate in the prayer services. They provide an outlet for women to publicly worship God. They also allow women to pray as a group.

These groups, although originally accepted by rabbis, have recently come under attack. The rabbinate in Queens, New York, banned them. Rabbi Moshe Feinstein, one of the leading decisors of Jewish law of our generation, also wrote that they are forbidden.[1] The proponents of women's prayer groups decried these big bad rabbis who were trying (as usual) to stifle women's spiritual expression. We will now look at why these groups, which fulfill the letter of the law, have come under attack.

In a nutshell, these women's prayer groups violate the spirit of the law. Their rationale is based on a non-Jewish value system where that which is public is considered superior to that which is private. In effect, these groups take private prayers and conduct them in as public a manner as possible. Being in the highly visible role of prayer leader or Torah reader is considered a superior mode of worship. This is anathema to Jewish thought.

Some women feel more connected to God when they participate in this public way. However, the only true way to connect

1 *Iggerot Moshe, Orach Chaim* 4:49.

192

to God is not through doing what feels good but through performing mitzvot. The root of the word *mitzvah* is the same as for the word *tzavtah*, which means connection. Mitzvot are the only means by which we can form an authentic connection to God. There is no mitzvah to be a prayer leader or a Torah reader for men or women. The obligation for the men is only to be part of the minyan.

On the contrary, a woman should feel more connected to God in a minyan than in a woman's prayer group because she is able to recite all of the prayers.

One of the fallacies of American feminist philosophy, which is fortunately slowly changing but which women's prayer groups have adopted, is the assumption that anything traditionally associated with men is superior to anything traditionally associated with women. For example, a female truck driver would be lauded as a hero whereas a female nurse might be derided as someone who was brainwashed by the sexist society. This makes sense if perceived value is based on how closely one takes on traditionally male occupations. This is ridiculous when value is perceived by how much one does for others.

Women's prayer groups don't simply try to get women to participate in prayer, they try to mimic how men pray. Some women even wear prayer shawls like the men do. The way in which men pray is considered to be superior to the way in which women traditionally pray. In order to achieve "equality," women approximate, as closely as legally possible, how men pray. "Equality" is thought to mean "the same." Therefore, being as much like men as possible is how they will achieve equality with them. Prayer is then used not as a means of connecting to God but as a forum for airing their grievances. It becomes a way to use the letter of the law to violate the spirit of the law.

Another reason why current women's prayer groups are forbidden by these rabbis is that something which gives the appearance of being prohibited is itself prohibited.[1] For example, the reason that the combination of chicken and dairy is prohibited is because some people may think that the chicken is meat and conclude that the combination of meat and dairy is permitted. Women may not form a minyan for prayer, and they may not have *aliyot*. Women's prayer groups make it seem otherwise.

There is, however, nothing wrong with women getting together to pray. Women have been doing so for a long time, long before women's prayer groups started. Generally, women would get together in someone's home and say *Tehillim*, Psalms, on behalf of the sick in the community. Today in the communication age, women organize worldwide groups by having the members say the same prayers at the same time.

Morning Blessings

At the beginning of the morning prayer service is a series of blessings. One of the blessings that men say is "Blessed are You, Hashem, our God, King of the universe, for not having made me a woman." Women end the blessing with "for having made me according to His will." This has been used to illustrate just how misogynistic Judaism is. However, it is important to understand how this blessing was viewed by the Sages.

The Sages discuss this blessing as the third in a set of three.[2] The first blessing thanks God for not making the person a non-Jew. The second blessing thanks God for not making him a slave to a Jew. A non-Jew has the fewest commandments. When a Jew

---

1   *Beit Yosef* to Tur, *Yoreh Dei'ah* 242, and *Shulchan Aruch, Yoreh Dei'ah* 242:10.
2   *Tosefta, Berachot* 6:23, as quoted in Meiselman, *Jewish Woman in Jewish Law,* 49.

acquires a slave, the slave undergoes a partial conversion. The slave then has many more commandments than when he was a non-Jew. A free Jewish woman is obligated in all of the commandments, but she is exempt from some of them. A free Jewish man has the maximal level of obligation in commandments. With these three blessings, the man is thanking God for having the most commandments.

It is interesting to note how men do not thank God for this. They do not say "Blessed are You, Hashem...for having made me a man." Instead, it is stated in the negative, "for not having made me a woman." The word used for woman is *ishah*. If the blessing was just about thanking God for not having been made female, and have to endure all the extra pain that comes with it, then the word used would have been *nekeivah*, which means female. The word *ishah* denotes not just a female human being, but a righteous woman. Likewise, an *ish* denotes a righteous man.[1] It would be quite presumptuous for a man to bless God for making him an *ish*, for who is he to assume that he is righteous? He must therefore state the blessing in a more roundabout way.

A woman thanks God for making her "according to His will." What exactly does that mean? And why does it mean being exempt from certain commandments? In Genesis, we read how God gave humankind two blessings or gifts. One is *kibbush* — the gift of conquest, power, and grasping. This is referred to in Genesis 1:28, "Be fruitful and multiply and replenish the earth and subdue it, and have dominion over the fish of the sea and over the fowl of the air and over every living thing that creeps upon the earth." The gift of *kibbush* was given to men.[2] The sec-

---

1   Rashi on Numbers 13:3.
2   Rabbi Aron Soloveitchik, *Duties of the Heart, Duties of the Mind* (Jerusalem Press, 1991), 94–95.

ond gift is that of *chazakah*, which is reaching out to people and things through compassion, love, consideration, and guidance. It is referred to in Genesis 2:15, "And God took the Adam and placed him into the Garden of Eden to cultivate it and keep it." This gift was given to all women and to the men of the tribe of Levi.[1]

Kibbush is necessary for all progress. However, it is only a gift when it is used in a positive manner, such as for technological advances that help people. People are forbidden to couple this gift with the philosophy that "might makes right" and behave in a rapacious manner. We all know only too well how men can use their gift in a destructive manner. Therefore, they need the extra commandments to prevent them from abusing this gift and to help them channel it in a constructive way.[2] *Kibbush* will not be able to establish a paradise on earth unless it is paired with *chazakah*. It is not enough to conquer evil; one must also nurture the good. Note that the root of the word *chazakah* is the same as the root for strong, *chazak*.

Kibbush and *chazakah* are not only different activities, but can also be two motivations for the same activity. For example, Rabbi Manis Friedman gives the example of violence in males and females.[3] A male is violent usually because he wants to get something which isn't his. A female is violent because she is protecting what is hers. There is nothing more vicious than a mother whose young are threatened.

Chazakah is a more arduous but a permanent way to attain a goal, while *kibbush* is a somewhat easier yet temporary way.[4] For example, if a parent wants her child to do something she

---

1   Ibid., 95.
2   Ibid., 96.
3   Manis Friedman, *Beyond the Male Ego* (cassette tape).
4   Soloveitchik, *Duties of the Heart*, 166–167.

may force her will on him, or she can try to change his will so it accords with hers. Both approaches have their advantages and are appropriate at different times. However, when the child leaves the parent's house he will abandon whatever was taught to him only through *kibbush*, and keep what was instilled in him through *chazakah*.

Whereas now we need both *kibbush* and *chazakah*, during the Messianic Era everyone will be involved only with *chazakah*. Therefore, the woman's role is more in line with the Messianic ideal. It is for this reason that she thanks God for making her "according to His will" – that is His will of how ultimately the world will be.

An event that illustrates how both the man and woman can be happy with their respective blessings and roles in life is a ceremony called "*pidyon haben*" – the redemption of the firstborn son.[1] This occurs when the baby is thirty-one days old. Originally, the firstborn males of every family were to be the priests of Israel. Due to the sin of the golden calf, they forever lost this privilege and it went instead to Aaron and his male descendants, who became the *kohanim*. Therefore, a *kohein* who is not a firstborn is really standing in place of a firstborn non-*kohein* male.[2] The boy must therefore be redeemed of his responsibilities, which he cannot perform.[3] This is done by giving a *kohein* five silver shekels in exchange for the boy. Nowadays, people pur-

---

1 The father must be neither a *kohein* nor a *levi*, since Levites served in the Temple as well. The son must be the first child of the mother and born in a natural way. If the woman had a previous pregnancy which lasted more than forty days or if the boy was born via cesarean section, then he would not have been a *kohein* and therefore does not have this ceremony.

2 If the mother is a daughter of a *kohein* or a *levi*, then the boy is exempt from this ritual.

3 If the boy is not redeemed, then he must redeem himself when he is thirteen years old.

chase a set of five silver coins from a synagogue or a *kohein* to use in this ceremony.

One would think that this was a sad event because it reminds everyone of the sin of the golden calf and the tragic result which continues to this day. However, it is a joyous occasion. Although it certainly is an honor to be a *kohein*, there are many commandments which the *kohanim* are not allowed to perform because it would interfere with their duties. For example, *kohanim* are not allowed to have contact with dead bodies.[1] This means that they may not take part in any of the preparations of burying the dead. This is the mitzvah which exemplifies the ultimate level of loving kindness since the dead cannot repay the person. It also means that they are forbidden from certain professions such as being emergency room doctors, where they would regularly have to come in contact with death.

At the *pidyon haben*, people are celebrating the fact that this baby boy will be able to fulfill many commandments which he otherwise would not be able to. The *kohanim* are also happy because they have their own special mission. Likewise, in the morning blessings men are thanking God for being able to do the maximum number of commandments. Women are expressing gratitude for being given their own crucial mission, even if it means being exempt from certain commandments.

Making Prayer Meaningful

A lot of this chapter so far has concentrated on all the things

---

1   Exceptions to this are when there is a dead body found and there is no one else who can bury it, and when the dead person is an immediate family member.

women cannot do and why. This is because it is the restrictions that a woman often encounters first. But understanding the restrictions and even accepting them does nothing for teaching a woman how to pray authentically.

Before we talk about how to make prayer meaningful, let us examine what it means to pray and what it does not mean. Praying is not about reciting prayers from a book. Many people think that if they go through all the motions of praying – saying the prayer, bowing, and so on, that they are actually praying. But they are not praying, they are acting – they are saying someone else's lines. And they are not doing a very good job of it, either. Good acting is when one puts herself into the words and "gets into the character." But God is not interested in our acting. He does not want us to present ourselves, either to Him or to ourselves, as something we are not.

Prayer is how we verbally communicate with God. It occurs in the context of a relationship that we work on throughout our lives. It may not seem like much of a conversation since we are the ones who are doing all the talking. What makes it a conversation is the faith that God is listening, and that He does talk back in the subtle ways we perceive Him directly involved in our lives. A person can pray in her own words, or she can use texts written by our Sages to help her articulate herself.

Verbal expression is a vital, irreplaceable part of any relationship. But sometimes, talk can be cheap. When is talk cheap? Imagine a husband who mistreats his wife, takes her for granted, and then says "I love you" whenever he wants something from her or when she gets too upset. Those words, "I love you," will be very hurtful to the wife because they are insincere, they are said for an ulterior purpose, and they are a mockery of her and the entire relationship. Likewise, when Jews mock

God's commandments, their prayers only add insult to injury. As it says in Isaiah, "And when you spread your hands [in prayer], I will hide my eyes from you; even if you were to increase prayer, I do not hear; your hands are full of blood."[1]

Now imagine a loving husband who is considerate, affectionate, eager to make his wife happy in any way he can. Even with all the wonderful things that he does for her, she still wants to hear those three precious words, "I love you." His verbal expression of their relationship cannot be replaced by any other act. It's not enough to show how he feels, he has to tell her. Likewise, especially when a person does all of God's commandments with joy, God desires her prayers. As it says in the Talmud, "God desires the prayers of the righteous."[2]

But a wife does not want to hear "I love you" all day long, even from the most wonderful husband. What she really wants is for him to share himself with her. She wants to know if something is troubling him. She wants to know if something is on his mind. She wants to share his happiness and sadness and wants to be there for him through everything. She wants them to be truly connected. But that can only happen if he talks to her. Even if she knows what he is thinking, good or bad, she wants him to tell her. God is the same way. He wants us to develop a relationship with Him. He doesn't need us to tell Him what we are thinking because He doesn't yet know, rather He wants to hear it from our own mouths. He wants us to connect with Him and share ourselves with Him.

The degree to which women were educated varied greatly through time and place. In many time periods in many places, women did not pray from a siddur, a prayer book, the standard

---

1   Isaiah 1:15.
2   *Yevamot* 64a.

Hebrew prayers. Instead, they would pour out their hearts to God in their own words. Women had, and still have, a great love for saying the Psalms. One reason is that the Psalms, or *Tehillim*, express more emotion than many of the standard prayers, and address God in more intimate ways. *Tehillim* allow a person to express themselves to God in all of life's situations — tragedy, joy, fear.

Another genre of liturgy which women used is *techinot*. These are prayers which were written for and sometimes by women in the vernacular. *Techinot* are very personal prayers structured around a woman's life cycle. There is a prayer for the beginning of the month, a holiday associated with women. There is a prayer for going to the *mikveh*, a prayer to be said the day of a son's circumcision, a prayer for a baby's first tooth(!). Each *techinah* is very intimate — each one welcomes God into every crevice of one's being. An excellent book of *techinot* is *Techina — A Voice from the Heart: A Collection of Jewish Women's Prayers* by Rachel Zakutinsky.[1]

For many observant Jews, prayer is unfortunately a lightning-fast recitation of fixed prayer services with barely a thought to what is actually being said. There are many factors which contribute to this tragedy, especially for men. Men are required to say the entire morning, afternoon, and evening services, preferably with a minyan. Weekday morning services are quite lengthy, and those on Shabbos and holidays are even more so. The reason for this is that through the centuries, more and more was added to the services. During the week, people are rushing to go to work and don't have time for lengthy praying. A

1 Rachel Zakutinsky, *Techina — A Voice from the Heart: A Collection of Jewish Women's Prayers* (Brooklyn, NY: Aura Press, 1992).

morning service at the usual pace takes about forty minutes. On Shabbat and holidays, if the services don't go quickly then the people praying will be late for lunch. Also, if one is physically able to do so, one may not eat before praying. Thus, even at the usual quick pace, a man will go till noon before eating anything.

One might think that the relatively short afternoon and evening services, which take about fifteen minutes on average, would be different. But when one recites the same text, every day, several times a day, it quickly becomes rote. One becomes like a preprogrammed robot, automatically saying the words and bowing one's head at the appropriate time. Even when one wants to concentrate on what she is saying, it is difficult because one has already developed a very strong habit of mumbling everything very quickly. This is a problem that affects everyone — even the greatest sages. None of this is anything new — prayer has been like this since the beginning of relying on a fixed text for daily prayer. An excellent book on sincerity in prayer throughout history till today, and what can be done about the lack of it, is *Kavvana: Directing the Heart in Jewish Prayer* by Seth Kadish.[1]

When women relied on their own personal prayers, whether they composed them, or recited Psalms or *techinot*, it is highly unlikely that sincerity was a problem. As women become more educated and pray using the standard Hebrew prayers, they quickly fall into the trap of praying hastily and mechanically. But how can educated women pray in a sincere manner without dropping the formal prayers? Actually, it is easier for women to do this than for men. First of all, we must be careful not to snobbishly look down on our foremothers for their sim-

---

1   Seth Kadish, *Kavvana: Directing the Heart in Jewish Prayer* (Northvale, NJ: Jason Aronson, Inc., 1997).

plicity, and instead try to learn from them what sincerity in prayer really means.

Women have much greater flexibility in prayer than men. We do not have to say the entire prayer service, but only certain key parts (the priority of which prayers a woman should recite are beyond the scope of this book). Therefore, a woman can tailor what she says to give her sufficient time to pray in a meaningful manner. Since a woman does not have to pray with a minyan, she does not have to worry about keeping up with prayer recited at a breakneck speed. If she does pray with a minyan, then she can skip some prayers to give her more time on the others, while still keeping up with the congregation.

Also, there are numerous places within the standard prayer service when one is allowed to insert one's own personal prayers. By giving herself more time, a woman can actually use these opportunities. In this way, a prayer is never the same two days in a row. This keeps it from being stale. It also guarantees that at least during part of the prayer, the woman will pay close attention to what she is saying and mean it. In this way, a woman can enhance both her fixed and personal prayers.

Prayer helps the person praying in numerous ways. In Hebrew, "to pray" is *l'hitpallel*. This is a self-reflexive verb which means "to judge oneself."[1] Psychotherapists have long understood the power that speech can have on the self. Just through talking, a person can learn about herself, arrive at solutions to problems she was having, heal old wounds, and grow to new heights. The problem with therapy, however, is that the person is always trapped in her own subjective understanding of Truth. Since God is the only One who knows absolute Truth, it is only through associating oneself with Him, studying His will as ex-

1   Rabbi Samson Raphael Hirsch, *Horeb*, 618.

pressed in the Torah, and performing His will by doing the commandments that one can go beyond her own limited understanding.

After the above discussion on the dismal failure of fixed prayer texts, one may legitimately ask, Why bother with them? Why not just compose all of one's prayers? The fixed prayers were not composed by poets, but by the greatest Torah scholars. These were men who were immersed in studying and living God's will. The prayers they wrote were designed to help the one praying *l'hitpallel* — to pray, to judge herself, to go beyond her own limited understanding and approach God.

As Rabbi Hirsch writes, "[P]rayer denotes a step out of active life, so as to gain a true judgment about oneself. It is an attempt to gain true knowledge about one's ego, about his relationship to God and the world, and of the relationship that God and the world have to himself. It strives to infuse the mind and heart with the power of such judgment, in such a manner to direct the mind and heart to an active life that is purified, strengthened and made more sublime."[1]

He also writes, "*Hith-palel* means to take the element of God's truth and make it penetrate all phases and conditions of our being and our lives. This allows our entire being to gain a degree of harmony in God."[2] Two excellent books on the standard prayer texts are *The Art of Jewish Prayer* by Rabbi Yitzchak Kirzner[3] and *The World of Prayer* by Rabbi Eli Munk.[4]

Each woman has an enormous power in prayer. The model

---

1   Ibid.

2   Rabbi Hirsch, commentary on Genesis 20:7.

3   Yitzchak Kirzner and Lisa Aiken, *The Art of Jewish Prayer* (Northvale, NJ: Jason Aronson, Inc., 1991).

4   Eli Munk, *The World of Prayer* (Jerusalem: Feldheim Publishers, 1963).

for the way in which one prays the *Amidah*, the central prayer of every service, is based on the supplications of a woman named Hannah.[1] She was barren for almost twenty years. Every year she went with her husband and his other wife and their children to Jerusalem for the pilgrimage holidays. Every year her husband would pray for her in the Sanctuary in Shiloh (the Temple had not been erected yet). Even though he was a great person, his prayers for her were not effective.

Finally, Hannah realized that she could not rely on an intermediary to pray for her and she went to pray at the Sanctuary herself. She prayed standing up, saying the prayers so softly that they could not be heard by others. Only her lips seemed to move. She prayed with such fervor and devotion that God answered her, and she gave birth to the prophet Samuel who would later crown David as King of Israel (whose son, King Solomon, would erect the Temple).

There are many levels of meaning to the prayers. There are numerous ways they can be interpreted. They hold so much for each of us. Each person can find some part that is immediately relevant to her at every stage in her life. If a woman concentrates on her performance, she will feel like the performer in prayer. The more she pours out her soul to God, the more aware she will be of His audience.

Personal Reflections

It says in the Torah that in order to learn Torah, you must first stumble in it. Prayer in the synagogue is where I stumbled first. It took me a long time to begin asking questions, then un-

---

1 I Samuel 1.

derstand the answers intellectually, then finally actually feel comfortable in a synagogue.

When I was beginning to ask questions about Orthodox Judaism, I felt like if the men's role could be likened to a car then they were given the BMW. Since I had very limited knowledge of "cars," I thought that the BMW was the only truly excellent car. Anything else would be, at best, second rate. With time, I learned that there are other cars that are just as good as a BMW, like a Mercedes. The "car" that I had, which I thought of so lowly at first, was a Mercedes. Furthermore, I realized that the Mercedes was a much better fit for me than a BMW could ever be.

When I first heard that women were exempt from certain mitzvot due to their obligations at home, I was a single college woman. I rolled my eyes and thought, *Whatever!* Then I got married and had a baby and then I actually had some of those obligations at home. You have no idea what "obligations at home" mean until you have a baby. My husband would come home in the evening to find me still in my pajamas, not because I was lazy but because night and day were just one long stretch of feedings, diaper changes, and naps. 2 A.M., 2 P.M. — it was all the same to me. And brush my teeth? Forget about it! This time I thought, *Thank God I don't have to go to minyan in the morning!* What if I had to? Not only would it be impossible, but it would also make me feel guilty that I didn't go. And what would that say about Judaism's priorities? That taking care of a small baby was less important than going to the synagogue? That worship only meant formal prayer? Like I said, Thank God!

Before I had a baby, one thing that still bothered me was why women were exempt from certain obligations which they would have difficulty performing during only a part of their lives. But when I am taking care of my baby, I think of the *kohanim*, the priests. They are forbidden from doing numerous mitzvot such as burying the dead. However, they served in the Temple only between the ages of twenty-five and fifty. Why couldn't they have observed the other commandments between ages thirteen and twenty-five and after age fifty? I think one of the reasons is that their serving in the Temple was not just *a* stage in their life, it was *the* stage of their life. It was the epitome of who they were and what they were able to contribute to the Jewish people. Likewise, creating a Jewish home is the most important contribution I can make; it is *the* stage of my life.

I wish I could end this section by telling you how I feel totally connected to God through prayer, and that what started out as a major stumbling block is now a smooth ride. But prayer is *avodah*, work. When I was becoming religious, I started to say the entire *Amidah* every day in Hebrew even though I didn't know anything about it. I was struggling slowly through words I did not understand, and not feeling at all like I was praying. The *Amidah*, I decided, was not something I was ready for just yet, and so I stopped saying it.

With time, as I felt more comfortable in other areas of observance, the gap that a lack of daily prayer left became very palpable. I "chanced" upon Rabbi Kirzner's book, *The Art of Jewish Prayer*, which beautifully and simply revealed the richness of the *Amidah*, blessing by blessing. After reading the book, I again started to pray the *Amidah* every day. At first I said it slowly, plodding through the words and feeling a little awkward. I looked forward to the time when I could say the whole thing with my eyes closed. Then, I thought, I would really feel like I was talking to God.

With time, I was able to sail through the prayer smoothly. Soon, my mouth became quite accustomed to saying all the words to the point that I did not have to look at the prayer book or even think about what I was saying. My *kavanah*, sincerity, promptly disappeared. Looking back, it was during the initial time when I had to put so much effort and devotion into saying the prayer when my prayer was at its best.

Eventually, I included the Shema with all its blessings in my prayers. I prayed every morning in Hebrew in a rote manner at neck-breaking speed. I tried many times to at least pay attention to what I was saying, but habit soon took over. Another obstacle was that the first thing I said, the blessing before the Shema, was the part of the prayer that I understood the least. By the time I actually got to the Shema, my mind was wandering. The underlying problem was my attitude. I thought that prayer was far superior when said in Hebrew and formal prayer was far superior to informal prayer. I have since discovered that these are only some opinions and there are many others. Most rabbis would agree that it is preferable to pray in a language you understand, and that informal prayers are a vital part of our relationship to God.

Since the baby came home, I haven't prayed formally at home. Instead, I say short personal prayers at random times. I am only now beginning to think how I would like to start to pray the *Amidah* again, and only the *Amidah* for now, this time with feeling.

Recently, I have been able to do this several times a week. In fact, writing this section provided me a much needed push to do this. After all, if I am going to write about making prayer meaningful, I should at least try to practice what I preach. I am saying the *Amidah* with more sincerity for several reasons. Having not been able to say it for so long, I appreciate the opportunity to say it now. This time, I make a point of saying the words loud enough so that I, and no one else, can hear. I used to just mumble under my breath, mostly mouthing the words. Saying it just above a whisper forces me to articulate each word, forces me to go slower, and allows me time to think about what I am saying. Finally, I include numerous personal petitions, combining the formal and the informal prayer into my own personal conversation with God.

So I'm still working on it.

Chapter 6

Where Do We Go
from Here?

Education

During the last century, women have expanded their participation in many areas of Jewish life. One area where women
have greatly advanced is in their Torah education. When
discussing Torah study for women, we must distinguish between two types of learning. One type is treating the Torah as a
Torat chayim, the teaching of life. Here one learns Torah in order
to know how to be a good Jew. The focus of this type of study is
the halachah that is applicable in one's day-to-day living, the
written Torah as well as the writings of the prophets and other
works on ethics. Both men and women are obligated in this
form of studying.

The other type of studying is unique to Judaism – this is *Torah lishmah*, learning Torah for its own sake. Here one learns for
the sake of learning. One learns about parts of the Torah which

may not be directly applicable to oneself, and one may even learn things which one already knows. The focus of this study is the Talmud – the intricacies of how the laws were derived and how they must be applied. It is the study itself which is the goal. This is something which is incumbent solely on the men. Men's obligation to study is unlike any other mitzvah. Whereas other mitzvot one can do and finish, Torah study has no end. Men are expected to make Torah study the focal point of their lives to the degree that it is possible, given their particular situation.

Torat chayim teaches us how we are to act. If this type of learning was too difficult for many people, then there would be many who would not be able to fulfill the commandments. However, God does not require us to do that which is impossible, and so this form of learning is made accessible to all. To successfully study Talmud, however, one is required to make a lifelong commitment of one's intellectual concentration, effort, and time.

Women are and always will be exempt from the mitzvah of *Torah lishmah*. A number of explanations have been offered for this exemption. One is due to their role as an *akeret habayit*, which ensures the survival of the Jewish people. If many women would devote themselves to Torah study like men must, then that would seriously endanger the next generation both physically and spiritually. The Torah would not do anyone much good if there weren't any Jews to observe it and study it. However, this exemption does not depend on the explanation, and it still stands regardless of how busy the woman is with running a household.

What has changed in the past century is what is considered *Torat chayim* for women. What aspects of the Torah does a woman need to know in order to live fully as a Jew? In the past, before modern appliances and indoor plumbing, the burdens of running a household were very great. Therefore, the main occupation of most women was housework and child care. Since most women did not work outside the home, their education concentrated on how to run a Jewish household. This included ritual laws such as how to observe the laws of kashrut, Shabbat, and *taharat hamishpachah*. It also included moral laws on giving charity, welcoming guests, refraining from gossip, and all the other aspects of how to treat other people. But most important, the goal of the woman's education was to inculcate in her the belief in and awe of God, the Holy One, blessed be He. In the ideal manner, the woman would obtain this form of education informally, in the home of her mother and/or mother-in-law.

Until modern times, this method of educating women was successful. There was a lot of variation in how girls were educated and how much they were taught. Remember that we are dealing with three thousand plus years of history that spans most of the globe. An excellent book on the history of women's education is *And All Your Children Shall Be Learned* by Shoshana Pantel Zolty.[1]

Because of the complexity of the Talmud, a little knowledge of it could be a dangerous thing. Imagine someone learning a little anatomy and then thinking that she could diagnose and treat various maladies. Due to the women's other responsibilities, the Sages assumed that she would not be able to dedicate herself properly to Talmud study. Instead, she might learn a little here, a little there. They feared that this limited and incomplete understanding would have dangerous consequences. She might as-

---

1   Shoshana Pantel Zolty, *And All Your Children Shall Be Learned: Women and the Study of Torah in Jewish Law and History* (Northvale, NJ: Jason Aronson, Inc., 1997).

sume that she could issue a legal decision for herself when she should have consulted a rabbi. She might misconstrue what she learned and come to ridicule the Talmud.

For this reason, the dominant attitude of the Sages toward women studying Talmud was that of Rabbi Eliezer ben Hyrcanus, who said, "He who teaches his daughter Torah teaches her *tiflut* [variously interpreted as 'distortions,' 'deviations,' or 'trivialities']."[1] Note that in the above statement, "Torah" refers specifically to the Talmud.

However, this attitude only applied to the general case where the woman either did not have the time or the inclination to study. Women were never actually prohibited from studying Talmud. If a woman demonstrated her dedication to study, then her father or others were allowed to teach her. Throughout Jewish history, there were individual female scholars. It is interesting to note where most of these women were educated – not in renegade schools aimed at defying tradition but in the leading rabbinic families of the generation!

Women's spiritual needs changed starting with the spread of the Enlightenment, when it became accepted for girls to get a formal secular elementary education. A secondary and college education also became a feasible reality for a growing number of women. Jews took advantage of this free secular education for their daughters, while the sons were sent to yeshivah. The girls broadened their intellectual horizons with their secular education, but for a century no efforts were made to provide them with a Jewish education of comparable sophistication. As a result, many women left the tradition, which became unfulfilling and seemed hopelessly anachronistic. (Men left Judaism at this time as well but not due to a lack of education.)

1 *Sotah* 3:4.

During the late nineteenth century, Rabbi Samson Raphael Hirsch championed the idea that it was possible to be both a member of society at large and a committed Jew. Unlike others who preached a similar idea before him, Rabbi Hirsch emphasized that it was the Torah which must take precedence over the demands of society. He emphasized the study of Torah as a means of raising the next generation of committed Jews. In other words, he emphasized the *Torat chayim* aspect of Torah study. Therefore, he established schools for girls as well as boys. (Talmud study was still for boys only.) This method of schooling became accepted by the Orthodox communities in western Europe but not in eastern Europe, where the Enlightenment had not yet arrived.

The Enlightenment did eventually reach eastern Europe with disastrous results to the Jewish youth.

> The older generation seemed to have withdrawn into a spiritual world of its own, unaware of the potential for tragedy among the children. Teenage girls, educated in Polish gymnasiums, yearned for modernity. Their mothers found fulfillment in prayer and simple faith; their brothers in the challenging world of yeshivah and Torah study. And the girls? They were left with the feeling that Jewish life was a burden and the Torah itself outmoded.[1]

Nobody saw this tragedy as clearly as Sarah Schenirer, a seamstress from Poland who even as a child was known for her exceptional interest in religious matters. She was appalled by how much women took care of their appearance and how little

---

1 Devora Rubin, ed., *Daughters of Destiny: Women Who Revolutionized Jewish Life and Torah Education* (New York: Mesorah Publications, Ltd., 1988), 169–170.

they took care of their souls. She was determined to establish schools for girls to counter this trend. Since this was a major innovation, she knew she needed the support of the greatest rabbis of the generation — which she got.

The reason for this change in the rabbis' attitude was that times had changed. Whereas before tradition and families were strong, now they had become weak. It was no longer the case that a woman could get a quality, fulfilling Jewish education at home. Also, women had become more educated, and they began working outside the home out of economic necessity. They were thus constantly exposed to a foreign value system. Their Jewish education had to be stepped up to meet their intellectual needs and to show them how the Torah was far superior to anything secular society had to offer.

The result of Sarah Schenirer's efforts was the establishment of Bais Yaakov schools, named after the House of Jacob — the way God referred to the Jewish women when telling Moses to teach them the Torah. In these schools girls could receive an excellent Jewish education. While Talmud study was not part of the curriculum, the girls did learn much of the oral tradition in the context of their other subjects. Bais Yaakov schools were accepted by most of the Orthodox community in eastern Europe and it became expected that all girls would receive a quality, formal Jewish education. Even the minority which objected to this innovation still established schools for girls, although the curriculum was not as broad.

Whether or not girls should study Talmud and to what extent is a question that is being discussed today. Some argue that girls should not because they would only be able to get a superficial understanding of it. Also, since Talmud study is of a very abstract nature, it would not fulfill girls, who find more meaning in a more relational type of learning. Others argue that women should use their God-given intellect to study Torah on the highest level that they are capable of. Also, today women engage their intellect considerably in all the secular fields and it would be counterproductive for them to have access to every form of knowledge except that of their own heritage.

There has been an explosion in women's desire to learn in all segments of the Orthodox community. There has been a proportional increase in opportunities for women to learn at every level and every age group. There has been an expansion of yeshivahs for girls, and post high school institutions of higher learning for women have been established. Individual synagogues are providing more classes for women as well as for both men and women. For women who want to learn but have many other obligations, one-day learning sessions are being organized by synagogues, yeshivahs, and national Jewish organizations such as the Orthodox Union.

As women get a more rigorous Jewish education, they must also have an understanding and appreciation for the woman's unique contribution to the world.

New Observances

Today's Jewish woman is confronted by many changes in traditional roles and observances. Some are responses to changes in the world around us and have been accepted by most traditional authorities, while others are far more controversial. Let's look at some of these changes and the Orthodox response to them.

Women are participating more in the public aspects of Jewish life. They are serving in key positions on the synagogue boards and are no longer limited to the sisterhood or ladies' auxiliary. As previously mentioned, women are also participating more in women's prayer groups.

Recently, two synagogues hired women as "interns." Their job is to do things which *rebbetzins*, rabbis' wives, have traditionally done: provide spiritual support for women, teach classes, visit female patients especially when a male visitor would be inappropriate, and provide a distinct female mode of leadership. What is revolutionary is that these women have a formal, paying job doing this. Proponents of this system say having a female intern allows a synagogue to fill this key role without burdening the *rebbetzin*.

Women are celebrating life-cycle events to a greater extent than in the past. The birth of a girl is celebrated by the entire community, whereas in the past it was a family affair. There are various customs as to how this is celebrated.

Becoming a bat mitzvah, almost a nonevent in the past, is celebrated as a key milestone in the girl's life. Again, we see a great variety in how this event is marked. In some communities there is a party at home with family and the girl's close friends. In other communities, the party is more elaborate and is attended by the women of the community. Yet in other communities, there is a lavish affair attended by the family, community, and friends. In most communities, the girl is expected to give a *d'var Torah*, a discourse on some topic in the Torah.

Women are also celebrating Rosh Chodesh more by forming "Rosh Chodesh groups." Rosh Chodesh is a minor Jewish holiday that occurs at the new moon which marks the beginning of the Hebrew month. This holiday was given to women as a reward for not participating in the sin of the golden calf. At these Rosh Chodesh groups women celebrate in various ways, such as by hearing a Torah lecture, going to a women's-only performance, or gathering to say *Tehillim* (Psalms).

As women increasingly learn directly from the sources of Jewish law, they are discovering commandments that have not been traditionally observed by women in the past, such as forming a *zimun*. When a person eats a meal with bread, she must say *Birkat HaMazon*, the blessing of thanksgiving. When at least three people of the same gender eat together, they can say the blessing as a group, with one member "inviting" the others to bless together. An additional phrase of praise to God is said as well. This group is called a *zimun*. While most halachic authorities hold that women may form a *zimun*,[1] it is still a rare practice today. Some women are also questioning certain observances that women have traditionally not taken part in, such as wearing tzitzit and tefillin.

The reaction to these developments in women's spiritual expression has varied greatly depending on the observance in question. For example, Rosh Chodesh groups have been accepted without question and receive the most support in the most traditional communities. There is some controversy over the appropriate way to celebrate the birth of a girl and the bat mitzvah, although most agree that a celebration is in order. At the other extreme, women's prayer groups and women wearing tzitzit or tefillin are vehemently opposed by almost all of the Jewish leaders and receive little support from Jewish women.

How is one to judge innovation in spiritual expression? The Torah itself provides us with guidelines. First let us revisit the story of Hannah. Every year she would go to the Sanctuary in

---

1 Rabbi Yitzchak Yaacov Fuchs, *Halichos Bas Yisrael: A Women's Guide to Jewish Observance*, vol. I (Southfield, MI: Targum Press, Inc., 1985), 65.

Shiloh with her husband, Elkanah, and his second and very fertile wife, Peninah. Every year Elkanah would pray for her and Peninah would taunt her. And in the following year, Hannah would again return to Shiloh, childless.

One year Elkanah became so frustrated with the situation that he said to Hannah, "Why do you cry and why do you not eat? Why is your heart broken? Am I not better to you than ten sons?"[1] At this point Hannah went to pray in the Sanctuary herself. She did this in an unusual manner. It was the custom to say prayers aloud. However, she said them very quietly so that it seemed that only her lips were moving. Eli the High Priest watched her and, noting her unusual manner, thought she was drunk.

> Eli said to her, "How long will you be drunk? Remove your wine from yourself!"
>
> Hannah answered, and said, "No, my lord, I am a woman of aggrieved spirit. I have drunk neither wine nor strong drink, and I have poured out my soul before God. Do not deem your maidservant to be a base woman — for it is out of much grievance and anger that I have spoken until now."
>
> Eli then answered, "Go in peace. The God of Israel will grant the request you have made of Him."[2]

Elkanah's remarks were meant to be consoling. However, Malbim notes that they had the opposite effect and prompted Hannah to go pray for herself. Elkanah reasoned that there were only two reasons to want children: to fulfill the commandment to procreate and to ensure that one would be supported in old

---

1   I Samuel 1:8.
2   Ibid., 14–17.

age. Since women are not obligated to have children, Elkanah thought Hannah was just concerned about her future material welfare. To this he responded that he could support her like ten sons. Today, some people, like Elkanah, are bewildered by the need for women to do things that they are not obligated to do. Hannah then realized that Elkanah could not pray for her effectively because he did not feel her pain. She realized that she had to go pray herself.

When Eli saw her unusual form of prayer, his initial reaction was to condemn her as a drunk. Likewise, today many people accuse women wrongly of being drunk on feminism when they request any changes. However, after Eli realized Hannah's sincerity, he told her to "go in peace."

Now let us look at the story of Nadav and Avihu, the sons of Aaron, who also worshiped God in an innovative way with disastrous results. The Jews, wandering in the desert after the sin of the golden calf, were commanded by God to build Him a Sanctuary. The Jews responded with wholehearted generosity — freely giving their most valuable possessions and participating in the building process to the best of their abilities. Finally, the Sanctuary was complete and the time had come to inaugurate it and all of its holy vessels. The inauguration service took seven days, and on the eighth day, Aaron and all of his sons were to be consecrated as *kohanim*, priests. In the middle of the consecration ceremony,

> The sons of Aaron, Nadav and Avihu, each took his fire pan. They put fire in them and placed incense upon it, and they brought before God an alien fire that He had not commanded them. A fire came forth from before God and consumed them, and they died before God.[1]

---

1 Leviticus 10:1–2.

What was Nadav and Avihu's sin that they were so punished? The key phrase is "They brought before God an alien fire that He had not commanded them." Note that the word for alien, *zarah*, is the same word that describes idolatry, *avodah zarah*, or "alien worship." Rabbi Yishmael states that the fire was alien because God had not commanded it.[1] He also states that they were drunk, and it is forbidden for a *kohein* to serve in the Temple while drunk.[2] Today, there are many women who really are drunk on a foreign value system and are attempting to inject this value system into Torah life.

Rabbi Akiva states that the fire was alien because it did not come from the altar, as the fire for the incense offering should have.[3] Rabbi Eliezer states that not only was the fire alien, but they made a legal decision in front of their teachers, Moses and Aaron, that this was indeed permitted. It is forbidden to rule on legal matters in the presence of one's Torah teachers and their doing so compounded their sin. While some women give a lot of lip service to being committed to the halachic process, they often sidestep the crucial part of this process: asking the leading rabbis about the appropriateness of new practices and then following their rulings.

Another opinion states that Nadav and Avihu offered the incense as a means to reciprocate the great love God had shown the Jewish people when He sent a Heavenly fire to consume their offering.[4] This demonstrates that noble intentions alone do not make an innovation permitted.

---

1   Rabbi Nosson Scherman and Rabbi Meir Zlotowitz, ed., *The Chumash* (New York: Mesorah Publications, Ltd., 1994), 593.
2   Ibid.
3   Ibid.
4   Ibid.

Finally, let us look at the daughters of Tzelafchad, who successfully petitioned Moses. It was toward the end of the Jews' journey in the desert, and the Land of Israel was being divided among the tribes. The land would be apportioned to men who were the heads of household at the beginning of the forty-year journey in the desert. However, each of those men had already died or would die before entering the Land of Israel because they listened to the negative report of the spies. The land that the men would have received instead would go to their sons. There was one man named Tzelafchad who had died leaving five daughters but no sons. It seemed that his share would get absorbed by his brothers.

> The daughters of Tzelafchad, son of Hepher, son of Gilead, son of Machir, son of Manasseh, of the families of Manasseh son of Joseph drew near — and these are the names of his daughters: Mahlah, Noah, Hoglah, Milcah, and Tirzah — and they stood before Moses, before Elazar the Kohein, and before the leaders and the entire assembly at the entrance to the Tent of Meeting, saying: "Our father died in the desert, but he was not among the assembly that was gathering against Hashem in the assembly of Korah, but he died of his own sin; and he had no son. Why should the name of our father be omitted from among his family because he had no son? Give us a possession among our father's brothers." And Moses brought their judgment before Hashem.
>
> Hashem said to Moses, saying, "The daughters of Tzelafchad speak properly. You shall surely give them a possession of inheritance among the brothers of

their father, and you shall cause the inheritance of their father to pass over to them. And to the children of Israel you shall speak, saying: 'If a man will die and he has no son, you shall cause his inheritance to pass over to his daughter.' "[1]

As Sarah Schneider expounds in her essay, "The Daughters of Tzlafchad: Towards a Methodology of Attitude Around Women's Issues,"[2] this passage in the Torah is quite relevant to questions of new observances. It teaches both women seeking halachic support for changes as well as the rabbis who are ruling on their questions the proper path to follow in order to promote a peaceful and productive discourse. Here we will highlight just a few of the points she raises. I urge the interested reader to read her original essay for a thorough treatment of this topic.

We are taught by the Sages, "The daughters of Tzelafchad were learned women. They presented their petition in a logical and halachically sophisticated manner."[3] Due to their love of God and their learning, they were able to present an argument to Moshe that was true both to the letter and the spirit of the law. In fact, their petition contained both the legal argument and its ruling. As it says, "And Moses brought their judgment before Hashem" — their *judgment* and not their question. Interestingly, there is no criticism from Moses or other rabbis for their assertiveness. Neither is there any sign that they felt threatened by their intellectual ability. Instead, the daughters of Tzelafchad re-

---

1 Numbers 27:1–8.
2 Sarah Schneider, "The Daughters of Tzlafchad: Towards a Methodology of Attitude Around Women's Issues," in *Torah of the Mothers*, eds. Ora W. Elper and Susan Handelman (Jerusalem: Urim Publications, 2000), 155–169.
3 *Bava Batra* 119b, *Devarim Rabbah* 21:11.

ceive unqualified praise for their actions.

The Midrash fills in for us a piece of the conversation that took place between Moses and the daughters of Tzelafchad:

> Daughters: Give us a portion of the land along with our fa-ther's brothers.
>
> Moses: It is impossible for a daughter to inherit.
>
> Daughters: Why?
>
> Moses: You are women.
>
> Daughters: Then let our mother enter into a levirate marriage and conceive an inheritor that way.
>
> Moses: Impossible. Once there are children, levirate marriage is not possible.
>
> Daughters: You are contradicting yourself, Moses. Ei-ther we are not seed and the obligation of levirate marriage applies to our mother, or we are seed and can inherit the land ourselves.
>
> At that moment they convinced Moses. When he heard the justice of their complaint he immediately pre-sented their case before God.[1]

Judaism does not change easily. This is what gives it its strength and integrity. At the same time, each Jew holds some piece of the Torah that only he or she can reveal, either directly or indirectly. This happens directly when one has a novel insight into the Torah. This happens indirectly when unique circum-stances arise in one's life that require a new application of halachah. The highest level is revealing a piece of the actual To-rah, as the daughters of Tzelafchad did.

When a non-Jew seeks to convert, he gets rejected at least three times. This is so that only those with true and pure motiva-

---

1 *Yalkut Shimoni* 773.

tions will enter the Jewish people. Likewise, every halachic innovation is like a convert which will also meet with initial resistance. It is this resistance which purifies the initial idea and ensures that only the true ideas get accepted. Moses refused the daughters of Tzelafchad three times before they convinced him of the justice of their claim.

"They trusted in the Merciful One, Master of the world... and came before Moses...and the entire congregation at the entrance to the Sanctuary."[1] The word used for trust is *yarchitzu*, which has the same root as *rachatz*, meaning "to cleanse." Once they presented their petition, they "cleansed" themselves of attachment to a favorable verdict, desiring only truth.

Here lies the crucial difference between women who seek changes to satisfy a feminist ideal and women who seek to live up to the Torah ideal. Both sets of women seek spiritual fulfillment, and they are both accused of being influenced by feminism. Whereas one group embraces feminism and labels themselves as Orthodox Jewish feminists, the other group vehemently denies any such association.

The difference between these two groups of women is whose will they want to be done. Orthodox Jewish feminists view feminism as their ideal, and try to change Judaism to fit this ideal as much as possible within the "confines" of halachah. While all feminists agree that women are equal to men, there is currently a debate on whether men and women are fundamentally different, or whether they are the same, with all differences being attributed to society. Orthodox Jewish feminists have taken the latter view and have championed such "equalizing" practices as women's prayer groups and the bride taking on as many of the customs traditionally performed by the groom as

1 *Targum Yonatan*, Numbers 27:1.

possible. Feminists want their own will to be done.

The other group of women views the Torah as their ideal and are using select feminist influences to help them achieve this ideal. The halachah is seen as providing guidelines and not as an annoying obstacle. Whenever there is a conflict between Torah values and feminist values, the Torah wins out because there is no contest. Only those elements of feminism that help women achieve the Torah way of life are used. Ultimately, it is God's will that they want to do. As much as they want a particular innovation, they don't want it even more if it is not the truth. As we embrace our heritage and go in the footsteps of our foremothers and beyond, we must make sure that our actions are for the sake of Heaven.

Just as the daughters of Tzelafchad teach us how people should approach making requests for innovation, likewise Moses teaches us how rabbis should respond to these requests.

Moses understood very well the desire for land in the Land of Israel, especially since he knew he would never set foot in it. He truly empathized with their cause and he prayed to God for a favorable judgment. "The Torah is teaching us the power of the tzaddik. The daughters of Tzelafchad presented their petition to Moshe [Moses]...and Moshe prayed to God to concede to their request and to permit them a portion in the land. God agreed to Moshe's prayer as the *midrash* says (Exodus Rabbah 21:2), 'Moshe commanded and God obeyed him.' "[1] This *midrash* implies that it was actually Moses' prayer that drew down the favorable ruling.

There are various opinions on how exactly Tzelafchad

1   *Me'or VeShemesh, Masai,* as quoted in Schneider, "Daughters of Tzlafchad," 167.

sinned. The *Zohar* draws a parallel between where he died, the desert or the *midbar*, and the word *midaber*, "to speak." It then concludes that his sin was speaking improperly against Moses.[1] His daughters were concerned that this would bias Moses against their claim and so brought this to his attention. Moses understood their concern and so brought the matter to God so that there would be no doubt as to the truth of the verdict.

As the *Zohar* continues to explain, "The daughters of Tzelafchad did not realize that because 'Moshe was the humblest man on all the earth' (Numbers 12:3) unlike the rest of mankind, he would not hold a grudge and his conflict with Tzelafchad would not have affected his legal judgment."[2] Nevertheless, the *Zohar* praises the daughters for what they did, and it praises Moses for accommodating their concern.

Ideally, when a judge has a personal interest in a case, he should excuse himself from judging it. True justice requires complete objectivity. Making changes in how women have traditionally observed Judaism is a very emotionally loaded topic in which everyone, men and women, have a personal interest. Since we do not have access to God's direct intervention, how do we go about making objective decisions in this very volatile area?

The Talmud teaches us how to find this place of objectivity within ourselves. We need to formulate logical and compelling reasons for *both* sides of an argument until we reach a place of "not knowing" what the correct verdict should be.[3] A master of

---

1 *Zohar*, Numbers 21:2–6, as quoted in Schneider, "Daughters of Tzlafchad," 164.

2 Ibid., as quoted in Schneider, "Daughters of Tzlafchad," 165.

3 See Jerusalem Talmud, *Sanhedrin* 21a–b: "Moses said to God, 'Master of the Universe, tell me the halachah about...?' God answered, 'The halachah is whatever the majority decides. If the majority acquits, so it is; if the

Torah was one who could formulate forty-nine reasons for and forty-nine reasons against.[1] It is not enough to simply list the pros and cons, one must really not know what the correct judgment should be. Until then, one's ego is still involved in the decision process. Only from this place of "not knowing" can we hope to make a ruling that is true to the Torah. As Sarah Schneider says, "From the place of true not-knowing, one selects the most spiritually productive solution for these circumstances and these times."[2]

"Seek to acquire an understanding heart that hears the words that prove unclean and the words that prove clean, those that prohibit and those that permit, those that disqualify and those that declare fit" (*Chagigah* 3b). When a rabbi is asked a halachic question, he must weigh both sides of the issue with complete impartiality and then reach a decision based on the Torah's dictates. Questions involving women taking on new observances are sometimes not so clear cut. Many factors come into play, most notably the women's intention. The rabbis need to use their "understanding hearts" in such cases to assist them in reaching the true Torah ruling on the issue.

Our leaders today have the awesome responsibility of deciding on women's petitions for changing a tradition that is

---

majority convicts, so it is.' This is in order that all of the Torah's possible interpretations of the question be elucidated, i.e., forty-nine that prove the object's purity, forty-nine that prove its impurity.... A sit says, 'The words of God are pure. Silver refined in a furnace upon the ground, purified sevens of times' (Psalms 12:7)" (quoted in Schneider, "Daughters of Tzlafchad," 166).

1   See *Sofrim* 16.7: "Rabbi Akiva had a distinguished disciple who knew how to interpret the Torah in forty-nine aspects of impurity and forty-nine aspects of purity, not one reason being the same as another.... Whence did he learn all these? He was learned in the Scriptures, expert in the Mishnah, distinguished in Talmud, and brilliant in Aggadah."

2   Schneider, "Daughters of Tzlafchad," 167.

thousands of years old. Women seeking change need to take their egos out of the discussion to the greatest extent possible and stay true to both the letter and spirit of the law. With the rabbis remaining completely impartial during their ruling and using their understanding hearts, they can root out anything that is antithetical to Torah values. When both sides approach each other with mutual respect, caring, and the desire to fulfill only God's will, then the discussions will enable God's will to be done and speed along the Messianic Era.

Personal Reflections

What does Judaism look like from "the other side" of the *mechitzah*? It drove me away in a rage. I vowed never to return, remember? I chose to be a Conservative prayer leader. Now, some may chuckle and think, *And look where she is now!* But I was not the only one who left, and the vast majority of the other women will not return.

So why did I choose to go back to the "other side" of the *mechitzah* when I could have been a prayer leader? It was because I discovered the rich tradition that, despite initial appearances, truly values who we are as women and what we do.

Epilogue

So far, this book has taken me three years to write. I have often rebuked myself for not being more efficient and not finishing it sooner. However, it was important that I started it when I did and that I am ending it now. When I started writing, I had recently come back from Israel. My experiences, my enthusiasm, my skepticism, and the problems I had with Orthodox Judaism were fresh in my mind. If I started this book anew today, I would not be able to write it. I'm too far removed from the challenges I had. I have gotten comfortable in this way of life, and I don't even notice things that had bothered me before. But it was also important that I continue to write for three years. When I started writing, I was single. Now I am a wife and a mother. What I wrote earlier as an intellectual explanation, I now stand behind with the conviction that can only be gained from experience.

Now I must ask myself, where do I go from here? Part of the answer is about fourteen pounds of deliciousness who is in the bedroom, finally asleep. Will I be a good mother? Will he grow up to be a mensch? Will I be able to put into practice everything

I learned? Will I be able to make my home a *mikdash me'at*? I hope so.

I will end this book by asking you, where will *you* go from here?

For Further Reading

The following are just some of my favorite books and is not at all a comprehensive list of the existing literature on women and Judaism.

Judaism – General

Schneider, Sarah. *A Still, Small Voice*. This is not a book but a correspondence course. It teaches about the main ideas in Judaism with brilliant clarity, penetrating depth, astounding beauty, and courageous honesty. You can get information about this course at www.amyisrael.co.il/smallvoice or e-mail smlvoice@netvision.net.il, or write to P. O. Box 14503, Jerusalem 91141, Israel.

Women in Judaism – General

Aiken, Lisa. *To Be a Jewish Woman*. Northvale, NJ: Jason Aronson, Inc., 1992. A comprehensive book on women in Judaism.

Frankiel, Tamar. *The Voice of Sarah: Feminine Spirituality and Traditional Judaism.* New York: Biblio Press, 1990. An insightful book of great Jewish women and the feminine aspects of Judaism.

Heller, Tzippora. *More Precious than Pearls.* Jerusalem: Feldheim Publishers, 1993. A line-by-line analysis of "A Woman of Valor," which reveals the richness of this section of Proverbs.

Zolty, Shoshana Pantel. *And All Your Children Shall Be Learned: Women and the Study of Torah in Jewish Law and History.* Northvale, NJ: Jason Aronson, Inc., 1997. The title says it all.

Introduction to Kabbalah

Kaplan, Aryeh. *Inner Space.* New York: Moznaim Publishing Corporation, 1990. With his lucid explanations, Rabbi Aryeh Kaplan introduces the reader to Kabbalah. This is a must read for anyone interested in the underlying structure of Judaism's worldview.

Modesty

Manolson, Gila. *The Magic Touch: A Candid Look at the Jewish Approach to Relationships.* Jerusalem: Har Nof Publications, 1992. The definitive book on the mitzvah of *shomer negiah,* the prohibition of touching someone of the opposite sex who is not an immediate relative. Believe it or not, this is fun to read.

Manolson, Gila. *Outside/Inside: A Fresh Look at Tzniut .*

Jerusalem: Targum/Feldheim, 1997. The definitive book on *tzeniut* written with great wisdom and humor.

Taharat HaMishpachah

Abramov, Tehilla, and Malka Touger. *The Secret of Jewish Femininity.* Southfield, MI: Targum Press, 1988. A practical guide to observing the laws of *taharat hamishpachah* written in a beautiful and easy-to-read manner.

Kaplan, Aryeh. *Waters of Eden.* New York: Union of Orthodox Jewish Congregations of America, 1982. This is a fascinating, in-depth look at the concepts of *taharah*, *tumah*, *mikveh*, and many other fundamental concepts in Judaism.

Lamm, Norman. *A Hedge of Roses.* Jerusalem: Feldheim Publishers, 1977. More insights into the laws of *taharat hamishpachah.*

Slonim, Rivkah. *Total Immersion: A Mikveh Anthology.* Northvale, NJ: Jason Aronson, Inc., 1993. A multi-faceted presentation of the *mikveh.*

Life Stages

Note: These are practical "how-to" books for traditional women, but they demonstrate the woman's roles as wife and mother better than any theoretical book can.

Finkelstein, Baruch, and Michal Finkelstein. *B'Sha'ah Tovah: The Jewish Woman's Clinical and Halachic Guide to Pregnancy and Childbirth.* Jerusalem: Feldheim Publishers, 1993. Practical guide to the physical and spiritual aspects of pregnancy.

Levi, Miriam. *More Effective Jewish Parenting.* Brooklyn, NY: Mesorah Publications, Ltd., 1998. Techniques every parent should know in raising happy children.

Radcliffe, Sarah Chana. *Aizer K'negdo: The Jewish Woman's Guide to Happiness in Marriage.* Southfield, MI: Targum Press, 1988. Techniques for building a happy marriage – a must read.

Radcliffe, Sarah Chana. *Akeres Habayis.* Southfield, MI: Targum Press, 1991. How a woman manages the house while raising one to ten kids. (Guess how many responsibilities she must have. That's right – one: keeping *shalom bayit.*)

Prayer

Kirzner, Yitzchak, and Lisa Aiken: *The Art of Jewish Prayer.* Northvale, NJ: Jason Aronson, Inc., 1991. An in-depth look at the *Amidah.* Reading this is the perfect beginning for praying meaningfully.

Munk, Eli. *The World of Prayer.* Jerusalem: Feldheim Publishers, 1963. Comprehensive explanation of the prayer services.

Zakutinsky, Rachel. *Techina – A Voice from the Heart: A Collection of Jewish Women's Prayers.* Brooklyn, NY: Aura Press, 1992. *Techinos* were prayers written for and sometimes by women. They were very popular up till this century when Yiddish and religion were forgotten by most Jews. These prayers are more attuned to women's lives and special events.